AN ESSAY ON PHILOSOPHICAL METHOD

AN ESSAY ON PHILOSOPHICAL METHOD

By

R. G. COLLINGWOOD

OXFORD
AT THE CLARENDON PRESS

Oxford University Press, Amen House, London E.C.4
GLASGOW NEW YORK TORONTO MELBOURNE WELLINGTON
BOMBAY CALCUTTA MADRAS KARACHI LAHORE DACCA
CAPE TOWN SALISBURY NAIROBI IBADAN ACCRA
KUALA LUMPUR HONG KONG

FIRST PUBLISHED 1933
REPRINTED LITHOGRAPHICALLY IN GREAT BRITAIN
AT THE UNIVERSITY PRESS, OXFORD
FROM SHEETS OF THE FIRST EDITION
1950
REPRINTED BY D. R. HILLMAN & SONS, LTD., FROME
1962

CONTENTS

I. INTRODUCTION

II. THE OVERLAP OF CLASSES

III. THE SCALE OF FORMS

VII. TWO SCEPTICAL POSITIONS

VIII. DEDUCTION AND INDUCTION

IX. THE IDEA OF SYSTEM

X. PHILOSOPHY AS A BRANCH OF LITERATURE

I
INTRODUCTION
§ 1

1. THERE are some things which we can do without understanding what we are doing; not only things which we do with our bodies, like locomotion and digestion, but even things which we do with our minds, like making a poem or recognizing a face. But when that which we do is in the nature of thinking, it begins to be desirable, if we are to do it well, that we should understand what we are trying to do. Scientific and historical thought could never go very far unless scientists and historians reflected on their own work, tried to understand what they were aiming at, and asked themselves how best to attain it. Most of all, this is true of philosophy. It is possible to raise and solve philosophical problems with no very clear idea of what philosophy is, what it is trying to do, and how it can best do it; but no great progress can be made until these questions have been asked and some answer to them given.

Philosophy, moreover, has this peculiarity, that reflection upon it is part of itself. The theory of poetry may or may not be of service to a poet—opinions on that question have differed—but it is no part of poetry. The theory of science and the theory of history are not parts of science and of history; if scientists and historians study these things, they study them not in their capacity as scientists or historians, but in their capacity as philosophers. But the theory of philosophy is itself a problem for philosophy; and not only a possible problem, but an inevitable problem, one which sooner or later it is bound to raise.

For these two reasons, both because it is among his proper subjects of study and because without it his chance of success in his other subjects is diminished, the philosopher is under an obligation to study the nature of philosophy itself. Towards that study the present essay is intended as a contribution; its primary purpose being to consider the question what philosophy is.

2. There are various lines by which that question might be approached. One of these would depend upon the relation between an object and the thought of it. Any special science, we might argue, must have something special to study, and whatever peculiarities it presents in aim and method must be due to peculiarities in its object; from this point of view it would appear that the most hopeful way of approaching our question is first to define the proper object of philosophical thought, and then to deduce from this definition the proper methods it should follow. But this line of approach would offer no hope of success except to a person convinced that he already possessed an adequate conception of this object; convinced, that is, that his philosophical thought had already reached its goal. To me at least, therefore, this path is closed; for though I believe that certain ways of philosophizing are more fruitful

than others, I know of no philosophy that is not a voyage of exploration whose end, the adequate knowledge of its proper object, remains as yet unreached.

A second way, which might be open even if the first were closed, depends on the relation between means and end. We might ask what kind of results philosophy hopes or desires to achieve; and, having thus laid down its programme, consider what means can be found of realizing it. But although every philosopher has some idea of what he hopes to achieve, this idea varies from person to person and in the same person from time to time; nor could it be otherwise, for any progress in thought must bring with it a certain change in the conception of its own end, the goal of one stage being the starting-point of the next. If I followed this method, therefore, I could not hope or even desire to command the assent of my readers, or even my own assent hereafter.

3. There remains a third line of approach. Philosophy never with any of us reaches its ultimate goal; and with its temporary gains it never rests content; *e pur si muove*: it is an activity which goes on in our minds, and we are able to distinguish it from among others, and to recognize it by certain peculiar marks. These marks characterize it as an activity or process; they are, therefore, peculiarities of procedure; and accordingly it is possible to answer the question what philosophy is by giving an account of philosophical method.

This suggests taking philosophical thought as a special kind of fact, scrutinizing it, and describing the procedure which it is found to exhibit. But that would not be enough. The question what philosophy is, cannot be separated from the question what philosophy ought to be. When we distinguish philosophy from the other activities of our minds, we do not think of it as something that merely happens in us like the circulation of the blood; we think of it as something we try to do, an activity which we are trying to bring into conformity with an idea of what it ought to be. Consequently, when we set out to give an account of philosophical method, what we are trying to describe is not so much a method actually followed by ourselves or any one else, as a method which in our philosophical work we are trying to follow, even if we never entirely succeed. Hence an account of philosophical method must attempt to satisfy two conditions. First, to avoid a kind of philosophical utopianism, it must keep in touch with facts, and never lose sight of the question what methods have actually been used by philosophers of the past. Secondly, to avoid replacing a philosophical question by an historical one, it must treat all such precedents as mere preliminaries to the main question: the final appeal must be to our own experience of philosophical work, and to our consciousness that when we are engaged in it these are the principles which we are trying to follow.

4. The problem of method is one which has exercised philosophers from the earliest times; but there are reasons for thinking it a problem of peculiar

importance to-day. Since the close of the Middle Ages there have been two great constructive movements in philosophy: the Cartesian, following upon the scepticism that dissolved the medieval systems of thought, and the Kantian, following upon the scepticism of the eighteenth century. Each was marked by a general agreement, such as must always exist in any period of achievement and progress, concerning the principles of method; and each was opened, and its main principles were laid down, by a methodological treatise. The movement of the seventeenth century is called Cartesian because its constitution and code of law were given to it by Descartes in the *Discours de la Méthode*; that of the late eighteenth and early nineteenth century stands in a similar relation to the *Critique of Pure Reason*.

The Kantian movement, as a philosophical movement, had worked itself out within fifty years from the publication of the *Critique*, and its influence passed into the sphere of historical and humanistic studies, as that of the Cartesian had passed into the sphere of natural science. Throughout the greater part of the nineteenth century, the attention of active minds was chiefly taken up by these two branches of knowledge, science and history; there seemed nothing left for philosophy to do, and it sank into complete neglect, except as an appendage of natural science or as a part of history. Late in the century a few men appeared in whom once more philosophy found its proper shape as a distinct and living form of thought. These men heralded the dawn of a new generation, that in which we now live, for which philosophy is among the universal interests of the mind. The ferment of a new growth is at work. In the quantity and quality of the philosophical books now issuing from the press of this country alone, our time can bear comparison with any other; judged by the number of writers, the seriousness of their aims, and their resolution in exploring new ways of thought, this generation has already reached a level in philosophical work which no one could have anticipated fifty years ago, and seems to promise a further advance which may even lead to a new constructive movement.

But in order that this promise should be redeemed, one thing is needed above all others: a patient and thorough reconsideration of the problem of method. The present is a time of crisis and chaos in philosophy. The exceptional difficulty which modern philosophers find in accepting each other's conclusions, and even in understanding each other's arguments, is a necessary consequence of their failure to agree upon principles of method, or even to find out exactly how they differ; this only is clear, that the old methods are no longer followed, and every one is free to invent a new one of his own. This is a state of things natural and proper to an age when new movements are in the making; but if it lasts too long discouragement and indifference will take the place of enterprise, and the new movement will be rotten before it is ripe.

There is a widespread interest in the problem of

method; but it has not yet been directly faced as a distinct problem, as Descartes faced it in the *Discours* or Kant in the *Critique*. Consequently philosophers of all schools are still in varying degrees, however little they may recognize it, under the domination of methodological ideas inherited from the nineteenth century, when philosophy was in various ways assimilated to the pattern of empirical science. If the state of philosophy at present is chaotic, that is because the rubbish left on the ground by the decayed systems of the last century is an impediment to sight and an obstacle to progress. The aim of this essay is to clear some of this rubbish from the ground, or at least to call attention to the need of doing so and invite others to go on with the work. To those who are busy constructing systems of their own, an invitation to take part in such elementary and menial work may seem an impertinence; but at least it betokens a conviction that beneath the apparent chaos there is unity of purpose and spirit, and that beyond the present crisis the future of philosophy is full of hope.

§ 2

5. The different parts of philosophy are so related among themselves that none of them can be discussed without raising problems belonging to the rest. The subject of this essay is the nature of philosophy; and it would be both easy and agreeable to expand this subject so as to include the place of philosophy among the other forms of thought,

the place of thought among the other activities of the mind, and the relation of mind to the world.

There are two reasons against yielding to this temptation. First, as a matter of principle: if the discussion of a special problem is allowed to expand until it becomes a discussion of the most general problems, no special problem will ever receive adequate attention; whatever question is raised will come to be regarded merely as a variant of the one ultimate question, and its special features will be neglected. The result will be a philosophy where all distinctions are swallowed up in a blank and colourless unity; a result no less fatal to the unity than to the distinctions, because the unity, which ought to be the articulated unity of an ordered system, has now become a mere undifferentiated chaos.

Secondly, as a matter of expediency. The purpose of this book is to call attention to a certain problem. There are plenty of books on the market in which the general problems of philosophy are ably and attractively dealt with, and I should hesitate to add to them; but there does seem to be a place for an essay on philosophical method; and the utility of such an essay can only be impaired if it expands into a general philosophical treatise.

For these reasons, though no doubt the thoughts here expressed have implications in metaphysics, logic, and the theory of knowledge, these implications will not be discussed. The reader will find that, in order to bring into relief the special characteristics of philosophy, it is constantly compared and contrasted with science, and in particular with two kinds of science, empirical and exact. He will also find references to history and to poetry. But he will find no sketch, however brief, of a general scheme in which poetry, history, science, and philosophy have each its own place.

6. Another warning is due to the reader at this point. I have illustrated the idea of exact science from elementary mathematics, and the idea of empirical science from zoology, botany, and other natural sciences. Perhaps a mathematician, if I am fortunate enough to number mathematicians among my readers, may say to me: 'Your account of the method used in exact science is altogether beside the mark; modern mathematical theory has changed all that, and you are tilting at a man of straw.' If so, I shall reply that my contentions, so far from being invalidated, are confirmed in precisely that quarter where confirmation is most welcome. For what I am discussing, when I distinguish philosophical method from that of exact science, is not mathematics itself but a certain method, often mistakenly used in philosophy, which is believed to be that of mathematics. Even if it is right in mathematics I believe it to be wrong in philosophy; but my attempt to combat it as a philosophical method may, I fear, be opposed by the reply: 'This method is so brilliantly successful in mathematics that philosophy cannot do wrong to imitate it.' That is an argument, I contend, in which the conclusion does not follow from the premiss; but my objection to it is only strengthened if the

premiss is pronounced untrue. A corresponding answer would apply to a scientist who objected to my account of inductive science.

§ 3

The scope of this essay does not require that it should be prefaced by even the briefest history of its problem; but it will be of service to consider a few points in that history, as especially instructive for my purpose. I propose to take four philosophers, Socrates, Plato, Descartes, and Kant, and to discuss their contributions to the theory of philosophical method; not asking what methods they actually used in their work, which is an entirely distinct question, but only what methods they explicitly claimed to be using or recommended for the use of others.

7. The central position in the history of Greek philosophy occupied by Socrates was undoubtedly connected with his contributions to method. The very existence of the word dialectic, which from his time down to the present day has stood for an important group of methodological conceptions, owes its origin to his technique in philosophical discussion; and when Aristotle asked himself what contribution Socrates had made to philosophy, he answered in terms implying that, in his opinion, Socrates was essentially the inventor of a method.

Socrates stated his own theory of his invention by saying that knowledge was to be sought within the mind, and brought to birth by a process of questioning. The contrast here insisted upon is the contrast between perceiving (αἴσθησις), regarded as the observation of things outside oneself, and thinking (νόησις), regarded as the discovery of what is within. Socrates showed that this second activity was common to two kinds of inquiry, which he does not seem to have distinguished in his theory of method: mathematics and ethics. His revolt against the study of nature was essentially a revolt against observation in favour of thought; and whereas mathematical method, as an example of thought, had already been discovered by his predecessors, his own discovery was that a similar method, for which he invented an appropriate technique, could be applied to ethical questions. This technique, as he himself recognized, depended on a principle which is of great importance to any theory of philosophical method: the principle that in a philosophical inquiry what we are trying to do is not to discover something of which until now we have been ignorant, but to know better something which in some sense we knew already; not to know it better in the sense of coming to know more about it, but to know it better in the sense of coming to know it in a different and better way—actually instead of potentially, or explicitly instead of implicitly, or in whatever terms the theory of knowledge chooses to express the difference: the difference itself has been a familiar fact ever since Socrates pointed it out.

8. It is true that philosophical thought resembles mathematical in the manner asserted by Socrates;

each is essentially not a way of observing facts, but a way of thinking. But a closer comparison between the method of mathematics and his own new method of dialectic would have shown him that, though similar up to a point, beyond that point they differ in an important way; and the evidence before us suggests that Socrates himself did not explicitly recognize this difference. Nothing is said about it in any writing earlier than Plato's *Republic*, where it is developed with unwonted explicitness in a well-known passage at the end of the sixth book; there is nothing about it in the *Phaedo*, where the intellectual autobiography of Socrates not only permits but one might almost say demands a reference to it, had such an important conception been Socratic in origin. Without dogmatizing, therefore, I propose to regard this doctrine as a Platonic development of the conceptions inherited from Socrates.

The passage in question is that in which a line is divided into four parts so that $a : b :: c : d :: a+b : c+d$. Here $a+b$ and $c+d$ are the worlds of thought (τὰ νοητά) and perception (here called τὰ ὁρατά), whose relation has been expounded in the *Phaedo*; so far we are doubtless on familiar Socratic ground. What Plato now wishes to point out is that a similar relation exists within the world of thought, between two orders of objects and two forms of thought corresponding to them, these forms of thought being dialectic and mathematics.

Whatever may be the unsolved obscurities of this famous passage, one thing is clear: that it expresses a view according to which dialectic and mathematics differ in method. The difference is stated by saying that in mathematics the mind 'goes from hypotheses not to a principle but to a conclusion', whereas in dialectic it 'goes from hypotheses to a non-hypothetical principle'; and this is further explained by saying that geometricians posit triangles and so forth as hypotheses, and admit no argument about them, but proceed on this basis to demonstrate their conclusions; whereas in dialectic we use hypotheses not as principles, but as the hypotheses which they are, employing them as stepping-stones to reach something which is not an hypothesis but the principle of everything.[1]

Mathematics and dialectic are so far alike that each begins with an hypothesis: 'Let so-and-so be assumed.' But in mathematics the hypothesis forms a barrier to all further thought in that direction: the rules of mathematical method do not allow us to ask 'Is this assumption true? Let us see what would follow if it were not.' Hence mathematics, although intellectual, is not intellectual *à outrance*; it is a way of thinking, but it is also a way of refusing to think.

[1] *Rep.* 509 D seqq. The passages paraphrased are: ψυχὴ ζητεῖν ἀναγκάζεται ἐξ ὑποθέσεων, οὐκ ἐπ' ἀρχὴν πορευομένη, ἀλλ' ἐπὶ τελευτήν, τὸ δ' αὖ ἕτερον ἐπ' ἀρχὴν ἀνυπόθετον ἐξ ὑποθέσεως ἰοῦσα (510 B). ὑποθέμενοι τό τε περιττὸν καὶ τὸ ἄρτιον κτλ. . . . οὐδένα λόγον οὔτε αὑτοῖς οὔτε ἄλλοις ἔτι ἀξιοῦσι περὶ αὐτῶν διδόναι ὡς παντὶ φανερῶν, ἐκ τούτων δ' ἀρχόμενοι τὰ λοιπὰ ἤδη διεξιόντες τελευτῶσιν ὁμολογουμένως ἐπὶ τοῦτο οὗ ἂν ἐπὶ σκέψιν ὁρμήσωσιν (510 C–D). τὰς ὑποθέσεις ποιούμενος οὐκ ἀρχάς, ἀλλὰ τῷ ὄντι ὑποθέσεις, οἷον ἐπιβάσεις τε καὶ ὁρμάς, ἵνα μέχρι τοῦ ἀνυποθέτου ἐπὶ τὴν τοῦ παντὸς ἀρχὴν ἰὼν κτλ. (511 B).

In dialectic we not only draw the consequences of our hypotheses, but we recollect that they are only hypotheses; that is, we are free to 'cancel the hypothesis',[1] or assume the opposite and see what follows from that. The purpose of this procedure is no doubt the same as that of Socrates' midwifery, to bring to light that knowledge which the mind already possesses concealed within it; and this is now defined as knowledge of a metaphysical first principle called the good.

Plato explicitly tells us in his Epistles (ii, vii) that he has never committed this knowledge to paper. But we do possess, in his dialogues, an unequalled series of studies in philosophical method,[2] from which it is easy to gather what exactly he meant by dialectic. The *Parmenides* may be taken as an example. Discounting the long introduction, the body of the dialogue comprises a series of sections each devoted to working out the implications of one metaphysical hypothesis, the subject-matter of these hypotheses being borrowed from the Parmenidean philosophy. The first hypothesis is that the One

[1] *Rep.* 533 C: τὰς ὑποθέσεις ἀναιροῦσα.

[2] Recent work on Plato, notably that of Professor A. E. Taylor and the late Professor Burnet, has made it impossible any longer to regard the dialogues as essentially statements of a philosophical position or series of positions; but the same authors' attempt to explain them as essentially studies in the history of thought does not to me at least carry conviction. Whatever else they may be, it seems clear that they were intended as models for the conduct of philosophical discussion, or essays in method. I am not sure whether or no I had the first suggestion of this idea, many years ago, from the conversation of Professor J. A. Smith.

is not many; the second, that the One exists; the third, that it is not one; the fourth, that it does not exist. Here each hypothesis is 'cancelled' in turn; thought pursues every path which it can discover, in whatever direction it leads.

Plato's contribution to the theory of philosophical method, then, or at any rate that contribution which for my present purpose may be credited to Plato, is the conception of philosophy as the one sphere in which thought moves with perfect freedom, bound by no limitations except those which it imposes upon itself for the duration of a single argument. Consequently thought, whose nature is exemplified imperfectly in the ideal of mathematics, is perfectly exemplified in that of philosophy; any one who thinks, and is determined to let nothing stop him from thinking, is a philosopher, and hence Plato is able to say that philosophy (διαλεκτική) is the same as thought (νόησις).

This is a conception of the highest importance, and fertile in good results for the theory and practice both of philosophy and of exact science, as the history of both abundantly demonstrates. But considered (as it must be for the purposes of this essay) merely as a conception of philosophy, it has two defects, or perhaps a single defect which may conveniently be stated in two ways. First, it is merely negative. It distinguishes philosophy from mathematics only by the removal of a restriction, with the result that philosophy is represented as a form of thought substantially akin to mathematics and differing only in its range. Secondly, it is never made clear how this exhaustive canvassing of every possible hypothesis can lead to the discovery of the metaphysical first principle. If mathematical reasoning cannot do this, why should reasoning of the same kind do it when merely widened in scope? Plato may assure us, and we may agree, that the desired result does in practice follow; but we are investigating, not his actual achievements in philosophy, but his expressed theory of the method by which they were won; and in terms of that theory there is an evident gap between the idea of the means and the idea of the end.

However highly Plato's philosophical achievements are rated, and to rate them at any value short of the highest would be to confess oneself no philosopher, his theory of method must be admitted defective through failure to drive deep enough the distinction established by himself between philosophy and mathematics. The result is that his methodology splits philosophy into two parts: one an arid waste of ingenious logic-chopping, the other an intuitive vision of ultimate reality. That the first is in fact a pathway to the second may be vouched for by the experience of many generations that have taken Plato for their guide; but even if it is, we are here engaged on a philosophical quest, in search not of facts to be accepted on authority but of conceptions in whose light the facts may be understood; and these Plato has not given us.

9. In their character as men, there was little

resemblance between Socrates and Descartes; yet there is a remarkable analogy between their positions in the history of ancient and modern thought. Each closed a period of division and doubt, and initiated one of brilliant constructive progress, by the discovery of a method; each was driven to this discovery by a thorough study of what passed for knowledge in his own day and a resulting sense of his own ignorance; each in consequence resolved to distinguish observation from thought, and to make a new beginning by looking for truth within himself; and each found the clue to his new method in the principles of mathematics.[1]

Socrates had found in mathematics a model for dialectical reasoning; Descartes, disgusted with the dialectic of the schools, went back to the same model, and described the lessons he learnt there under four heads: the canons of evidence, division, order, and exhaustion. Nothing was to be assented to, unless evidently known to be true; every subject-matter was to be divided into the smallest possible parts, each to be dealt with separately; each part was to be considered in its right order, the simplest first; and no part was to be omitted in reviewing the whole.[2]

It was from the study of mathematics that Descartes learnt these rules, and it was to the advancement of mathematics that he first applied them; but he hoped from the first that they would prove useful in a far wider sphere, and by degrees he applied

[1] *Discours de la Méthode*, *première partie*.

[2] Ibid., *deuxième partie*.

them to the whole field of knowledge as he conceived it: that is, not only to mathematics but to metaphysics and the sciences of nature; for divinity he ruled out as a matter of faith, poetry he considered a gift rather than a fruit of study, and history he regarded as a pastime full of interest and not devoid of profit, but very far from the dignity or utility of a science.[1]

Whatever may have been the method actually used by Descartes in his philosophical inquiries—that, I repeat, is another question—it is clear that the method which in this critical pronouncement he claimed to be using was at all points identical with that which he used in mathematics. He admits only one method for all three branches of science; the problem of a special method appropriate to philosophy is one which he has not raised.

The philosophers who, in spite of his own modest disclaimer, treated his *Discours* as a system of precepts, found them highly profitable. Especially at a time like his, when philosophical doctrines had been reduced by probabilism to mere matters of opinion, nothing but good could come of insisting that they must be either based on solid argument or abandoned as indefensible conjectures. Hardly less beneficial was Descartes's second rule, that difficulties must be divided up and their elements considered separately, when this rule was taken in conjunction with the third, that they must be considered in their right order, and the fourth, that no element must be

[1] *Discours de la Méthode, première partie, deuxième partie.*

omitted. The magnificent philosophical work done in the seventeenth century was due not so much to its being a century of genius—*car ce n'est pas assez d'avoir l'esprit bon, mais le principal est de l'appliquer bien*—as to its being a century in which the Cartesian rules of method were attentively observed.

Yet, as both Descartes and his successors very well knew, philosophy and mathematics are, even in method, not at all points identical; and accordingly the benefits that philosophy can receive from an insistence upon their likeness are only partial. The great seventeenth-century philosophers, Descartes himself as much as any, in practice to some extent recognized the differences which in the *Discours* had been overlooked or implicitly denied. But that denial was not only a symptom that these differences were insufficiently apprehended; it was also an encouragement to overlook them, which reacted on philosophy itself by holding up to it a distorted picture of what it ought to be; and it was this reaction that set his problem to Kant.

10. Of the three Cartesian sciences, mathematics, science of nature, and metaphysics, to all of which Descartes had proposed to apply one and the same method, Kant, a century and a half later, could see that not all had profited equally. The Cartesian mathematics had stood firm, and continued to advance; the Cartesian natural science had undergone a good deal of criticism, notably at the hands of Newton; and the Cartesian metaphysics had worked itself into a blind alley. The inference was that

Descartes's method, as stated by himself, was adequate to the case of mathematics, but required modification in natural science, where it showed insufficient grasp of the significance of experiment, and still more modification in the case of metaphysics.

Some of Kant's younger contemporaries and successors ascribed to him the design of discrediting metaphysics for ever. It was a misconception both of what he intended to do and of what he did; but there was an excuse for it. Kant initiated a new kind of philosophy, as he thought, which he called transcendental or critical philosophy; its purpose was to serve as a propaedeutic or introduction to metaphysics, to warn the metaphysician against fallacies of method and to set him on the right road. It was in fact essentially a methodology of metaphysics. Having mastered the propaedeutic, Kant assumed that the philosopher would go back to his proper work, that of metaphysical speculation; and that now, having learnt its proper method, metaphysics, reformed and reorganized, would advance with the same sure tread as mathematics and the science of nature.

On Kant's programme, therefore, there were in future to be two distinct philosophies: a methodology, which he conceived himself to have given to the world in a definitive shape, and a substantive philosophy which, guided by this methodology, would be able to progress indefinitely. But this division, however attractive at first sight, was soon found unsatisfying. So far from being definitive, the

Critique of Pure Reason brought the problems of methodology into the focus of men's thought, and gave rise to discussions which to some extent diverted them from metaphysics and for a time made that appear a dead subject; and even Kant himself was not clear in his own mind about the relation between the two things, for he saw that in one sense critical philosophy was a part of metaphysics, though in another it was an introduction to it.[1]

He had impaled himself on the horns of a dilemma. If the methodology of philosophy (*Kritik*) is a propaedeutic to philosophy itself (*Metaphysik*), the name of philosophical science (*Wissenschaft*) cannot belong to them both; and we get the result, either that this name must be denied to the *Critique of Pure Reason* itself, a paradox rightly rejected by Kant's followers, or that it belongs exclusively to the propaedeutic and must be denied to substantive philosophy, which was from Kant's own point of view still more paradoxical. But on the other alternative, if methodology is a part of philosophy, Kant's programme collapses; for we can no longer hope to settle the methodological problems once for all and then go on with the substantive philosophy, because any advance in that will react upon and reopen the problems of methodology.

For this reason we cannot look to Kant for a

[1] *K.R.V.* A 841, B 869: 'die Philosophie der reinen Vernunft ist nun entweder Propädeutik (Vorübung), welche . . . heisst Kritik, oder zweitens das System der reinen Vernunft (Wissenschaft) . . . [welche] heisst Metaphysik; wiewohl dieser Name auch der ganzen reinen Philosophie mit Inbegriff der Kritik gegeben werden kann.'

satisfactory theory of philosophical method. What he has to teach us on that subject will fall into two parts which he tries, but without success, to keep in two watertight compartments: one relating to the principles and methods of transcendental philosophy and taught chiefly by example, the other to those of metaphysics, taught by precept in the concluding chapters of the *Critique*.

Bearing this in mind, we may turn to these chapters in order to see how Kant, at the end of his critical inquiry, sums up his conclusions as to the method of metaphysics. At once we see that his aim is not so much to controvert but rather to correct Descartes, by a careful distinction between philosophical and mathematical thinking. He argues in detail that, of the special marks of mathematical science, not one is to be found in philosophy, and that the adoption of mathematical methods there can do nothing but harm.[1] Philosophy knows no definitions: or rather, their place in philosophy is not at the beginning of an inquiry but at the end; for we can philosophize without them, and if this were not so we could not philosophize at all.[2] Philosophy knows no axioms: no truths, there, are self-evident, any two concepts must be discursively connected by means of a third.[3] Philosophy knows no demonstrations: its proofs are not demonstrative but acroamatic; in other words, the difference between mathematical proof and philosophical is that in the former you proceed from point to point in a chain of

[1] A 726, B 754. [2] A 727, B 755. [3] A 732, B 761.

grounds and consequents, in the latter you must always be ready to go back and revise your premisses when errors, undetected in them, reveal themselves in the conclusion.[1]

From this admirably clear and conclusive series of distinctions, Kant turns to discuss the principles of philosophical controversy. That reason has the right to criticize every opinion and discuss every subject with perfect freedom he proclaims with emphasis; but these discussions, he thinks, are bound to end in antinomies from which reason can find no issue. They cannot even be resolved, like the antinomies of the understanding, by reflecting that the objects to which they relate are mere phenomena; for they are not; they are things in themselves.[2] In this situation, what we must do is to accept those propositions which are 'consistent with the speculative interest of our reason'; for example, the existence of God and the freedom of the will; sceptical attacks on these propositions, therefore, are not to be feared, and should, indeed, be encouraged for the exercise which they give to the powers of thought.

I have quoted this passage in order to illustrate the confusions into which Kant is betrayed by his failure to think out the relation between critical philosophy and metaphysics. His plea for liberty of discussion in metaphysics rings true; but his reason for defending it destroys the incentive to it; for he argues that it can do no harm, since it can come to

[1] A 734, B 762. [2] A 741, B 769.

no conclusion. Why then should we pursue it? Because, says Kant, it is a useful gymnastic, in which reason comes to know itself better. This amounts to saying that the true end of reason is to come to a knowledge of itself, to become aware of its own power and limitations, in a word to master the lessons of the critical philosophy, and that metaphysical argument is of value only as an introduction to this.

The relation between the two kinds of philosophy has here suffered a complete inversion: originally criticism was to be the propaedeutic to metaphysics and give it the means of progressing; here metaphysics is the propaedeutic to criticism, and expires when criticism appears on the scene; for, as Kant himself remarks, the growth of criticism is bound to bring metaphysical controversy to a close. Neither of these two opposing views, taken by itself, truly represents Kant's thought. But they cannot be reconciled except at the cost of revising everything he has told us about the relation between his two kinds of philosophy.

The philosophical work of Kant is one of those things whose magnitude only seems to increase with every advance in our understanding of them; it bestrides the world, even now, like a colossus, or like a mountain whose waters irrigate every little garden of thought in the plains beneath it. And the problem of philosophical methodology was the central problem of his life. Yet he left this problem to posterity, not conquered, but only, as Caesar left Britain, indicated. So long as he confines himself to drawing the distinction between philosophical method and mathematical, his touch is that of a master; every point is firm, every line conclusive. But when he turns to give a positive account of what philosophy is, his own distinction between a critical propaedeutic and a substantive metaphysics, hardened into a separation between two bodies of thought, becomes a rock on which his argument splits. Even so, he went immeasurably beyond any of his predecessors in the direction of a true theory of philosophy. He solved rightly the problem which Plato had solved wrongly, the problem of the methodological difference between philosophy and mathematics, and so laid a firm foundation for all future inquiries into the nature of philosophical method.

II
THE OVERLAP OF CLASSES

§ 1

1. HISTORICAL thought concerns itself with something individual, scientific thought with something universal; and in this respect philosophy is more like science than history, for it likewise is concerned with something universal: truth as such, not this or that truth; art as such, not this or that work of art. In the same way exact science considers the circle as such, not this or that individual instance of it; and empirical science considers man as such, not, like history, this man as distinct from that.

It is therefore clear that, up to a point, philosophy has something in common with science, whether exact or empirical. But it is not clear how far the resemblance extends or what differences lie beyond it. To make some progress towards answering that question is the purpose of this essay; and, dividing the problem into parts and beginning with the simplest, I shall first consider what, in the statement that philosophy is concerned with the universal, is meant by the word universal.

To give an account of the universal, or, as it is also called, the concept, is the business of logic; but we cannot here content ourselves with simply accepting what logical text-books have to say on the matter. We have a special question to ask: whether there are any differences between the concepts found in philosophy and those found in science, whether exact or empirical, and if so what they are. The ordinary text-books of logic assume that there are none; that a concept is always a concept, and that any theory which adequately describes the concepts of science will adequately describe those of philosophy also. But our task involves reconsidering that assumption; for once it is admitted that there may be differences of some kind between philosophy and science, and that these differences may affect their methods, we cannot be too careful in considering how far they go and how deeply they affect the logical structure of these two kinds of thought.

It will be best, then, to begin by considering what account of the concept is given by traditional logic, and asking whether this requires modification in the special case of the concepts found in philosophy.

Traditional logic regards the concept as uniting a number of different things into a class. The members of the class are not merely grouped together, they are united by sharing a common characteristic, and are thus all members of the class only because they are all instances of the concept. The concept unites in itself two distinct kinds of plurality: first, the plurality of its individual instances, and secondly, the plurality of its specific differentiations. Thus the concept colour unites all the individual colours of all individual coloured things into a class of which they are members; but it also unites the specific colours red, orange, yellow, green, and so forth into a genus of which they are species. It may be convenient to refer to the former unification by saying that the concept is general, to the latter by saying that it is generic.

The logical doctrine of classification and division, as it stands in the ordinary text-books, implies a certain definite connexion between these two characteristics of the concept: namely, that if a genus is distinguished into a certain number of species, the class of its instances can be correspondingly divided into an equal number of sub-classes. Each sub-class will comprise the instances of one specific concept; the totality of the sub-classes will comprise those of the generic concept. Thus every individual present in the generic class will be present in one, and only one, of the specific classes, which are thus exclusive in relation to each other and exhaustive in relation to the generic class.

Logicians sometimes assume that this follows necessarily from the nature of the concept, and therefore applies universally to every concept whatever. But this is not the case. From the fact that a certain generic nature may be realized in various specific ways, it does not follow that no instance can realize it in two of these ways at once. For example, a work of art as such has a generic nature, which is differently realized in the specific natures of poetry and music. How, then, are we to classify a song? Common sense would rebel against calling it two separate works of art, a poem and a piece of music, going on at once; and it would be even more paradoxical to describe it as a third species, neither music nor poetry; nothing will serve but to say that it is both poetry and music, a single work of art containing the two specific forms.

2. Some logicians, recognizing this, treat the doctrine of classification and division not as the statement of a necessary element in the theory of the concept but as the mere description of a special kind of thing called a classificatory system.

But classificatory systems are not things that may be constructed or dispensed with at pleasure. In mathematics, for example, they are invariably found. A line is either straight or curved; these are the two species into which the genus line is divided, and they are exclusive and exhaustive: no line can be both, and there is no third species. The mutual exclusiveness of the species is not destroyed by identifying the straight line with the arc of a circle whose radius is infinitely long; that identification only marks the criterion (infinite length of the radius) which transfers the instance from one class to the other; it does not cause a genuine overlap of the classes. Further, because the line can be divided in this way, plane figures can be divided in the same way into rectilinear and curvilinear; such figures as a semicircle forming, not an overlap of these two classes, but a third class in which the bounding lines are partly straight and partly curved. In general, the concepts of exact science strictly conform to the rules of classification and division as laid down by logicians. Upon this conformity the methods used in exact science depend as the *conditio sine qua non* of their validity.

3. The same general conformity appears in the concepts of empirical science. Natural history divides organisms into animals and vegetables; even if there are some doubtful cases on the frontier, still the two great kingdoms are in principle, and almost wholly in practice also, mutually exclusive. The animal kingdom again is divided into vertebrates and invertebrates; vertebrates into mammals, birds, reptiles, and fishes; and so forth. At every stage there is a division of one concept, a logical genus, into others, its logical species, which are mutually exclusive and together exhaust the genus. There are difficulties about doing this: border-line cases, where it seems arbitrary to assign the individual either to this species or to that; paradoxical cases, where according to the chosen criterion an individual falls in one species when, on all other grounds, it would naturally be assigned to another; and the constant problem of ensuring exhaustion of the genus without adding, in defiance of sound principle, a 'miscellaneous' species at the end of the list. There are even cases where two adjacent species seem to overlap; as with the amphibians, which can breathe both in air and in water; but these cases are exceptional and limited, and can be fitted into the general classificatory structure of the concept without damage to its solidity. These difficulties are peculiar to empirical science; in mathematical or exact science they do not arise, for there the divisions can be

carried out *a priori*, and in consequence the exclusiveness and exhaustiveness of the species are assured.

§ 2

4. The traditional theory of classification and division, however true it may be as an account of the logical structure of all concepts belonging to science, exact or empirical, must be modified in at least one important way before it can be applied to the concepts of philosophy. The specific classes of a philosophical genus do not exclude one another, they overlap one another. This overlap is not exceptional, it is normal; and it is not negligible in extent, it may reach formidable dimensions.

If this is true, it will have serious consequences. It will make a difference as to the precise sense in which these classes together exhaust the genus, for their 'togetherness' will be of a peculiar kind. It will even make a difference as to the sense in which they are species of a genus at all. But these questions must be deferred until the first point has been established. In the argument of this essay the overlap of classes is to serve as a clue to discovering the peculiarities that distinguish philosophical thought from scientific; and therefore it is important that I should convince the reader, if I can, of its reality; for although it is familiar in philosophy and also, as I have remarked, to common sense, it is a paradox from the point of view of science; and a reader trained chiefly in that field may be tempted to meet the assertion of its reality with a flat denial.

I shall therefore attempt to show, first, that the overlap of classes has long been recognized as a fact in the case of certain possibly exceptional concepts; secondly, that it seems characteristic of what I shall call the philosophical phase of concepts that have a dual significance, philosophical and non-philosophical; and thirdly, that it is a regular feature of the concepts which form the traditional subject-matter of the philosophical sciences.

5. There are certain concepts whose recalcitrance to the rules of classification has long been notorious. Aristotle, in the sixth chapter of the first book of the *Nicomachean Ethics*, undertakes to inquire into the logical characteristics of the concept goodness. It had already been laid down, whether first by himself or by his predecessors we need not ask, that in classifying concepts under more general concepts we come at last to ten *summa genera*, the most general concepts of all, the so-called categories. In this chapter Aristotle points out that goodness is predicable under all the categories. But this is incompatible with the theory of classification, by which any predicate (for example, blue) must come in its right place under one category and one only (in this case, quality). The inference is either that good is an equivocal term, an alternative which Aristotle considers and rightly rejects, or that it is a concept of a peculiar kind, which will not fit into the system of classification.

Later philosophers developed the point here made by Aristotle. There is a traditional formula, well known from its quotation by Spinoza, *omne ens est unum verum bonum*. These three predicates, unity, reality, and goodness, are assigned by traditional metaphysics to every *ens* or being. But if all concepts were arranged in a table of classification, each divided at each stage into mutually exclusive species, the highest term in the table would be the most abstract of all possible abstractions: simple, abstract being. If being has necessary determinations such as according to this doctrine unity, reality, and goodness are held to be, it follows that these determinations are somehow exempt from the rules of classification. Just as Aristotle showed that the concept of good overlaps or transcends or diffuses itself across the divisions of the categories, so, according to this traditional formula, there is a similar overlap or transcendence or diffusion in the concepts of unity and reality.

6. Something of the same kind happens whenever a concept having a dual significance enters upon its philosophical phase.

There are words which are used in two different ways, a philosophical and a scientific; but the words are not on that account equivocal; they undergo a regular and uniform change in meaning when they pass from one sphere to the other, and this change leaves something fundamental in their meaning unaltered, so that it is more appropriate to speak of two phases of a concept than two senses of a word.

For example, matter is a word used both in physics and in metaphysics; and the dual usage is so far from being an equivocation, that we can trace not only a general connexion between the physical and metaphysical notions of matter, in spite of the difference between them, but even a special connexion between a particular physical theory of matter and a particular metaphysical theory corresponding to it ; for example, the concept of matter in what may be called classical nineteenth-century materialism is the metaphysical counterpart of the scientific concept of matter in the classical Newtonian physics. The difference between the two phases of the concept is that in Newtonian physics matter is the name of a certain class of things, separate from other classes of things, such as minds, and appearances like colours or sounds depending for their existence on the mind to which they appear ; in materialistic metaphysics it is the name of reality as a whole, and every distinction like that between so-called matter and so-called mind is reduced to a distinction within matter itself.

Such cases are common. Mind, for the scientist, in this case the psychologist, is the name of one limited class of things outside which lie things of other kinds ; for the spiritualistic philosopher, it is a name, perhaps the best or only name, for all reality. Evolution, for the biologist, is the way in which species of living organisms came into being ; for the philosopher, it is either a thing of no philosophical interest or else a cosmic process at work wherever anything specific has its origin.

Even in concepts that have no strictly scientific

phase, a similar distinction can often be traced between a philosophical phase and a non-philosophical. Thus art, for the critic, is a highly specialized thing, limited to a small and select body of works outside which lie all the pot-boilers and failures of artists, and the inartistic expressions of everyday life; for the aesthetic philosopher, these too are art, which becomes a thread running all through the fabric of the mind's activity.

An extreme case of the same principle will become increasingly important as we go farther into our subject. Even words like concept, judgement, inference, though at first sight unambiguously philosophical, betray subtle distinctions of meaning according as they are applied to philosophical or non-philosophical thought; and these differences of meaning, one of which is already under examination in the present chapter, will be found to obey the same general law.

It appears from these instances that when a concept has a dual significance, philosophical and non-philosophical, in its non-philosophical phase it qualifies a limited part of reality, whereas in its philosophical it leaks or escapes out of these limits and invades the neighbouring regions, tending at last to colour our thought of reality as a whole. As a non-philosophical concept it observes the rules of classification, its instances forming a class separate from other classes; as a philosophical concept it breaks these rules, and the class of its instances overlaps those of its co-ordinate species.

This is a familiar fact. It is often held up as an

inherent vice of philosophical as opposed to scientific thinking. What concerns us is not the question whether it is a vice or a virtue, but the fact that it happens. That it happens sometimes, these instances show; and this is enough to prove it a danger with which philosophical thought must reckon if it adopts methods proper to science, where this feature does not exist. If it happens always, it is more than a danger; it is a clue to the peculiarities of philosophical thinking and the characteristics of a philosophical method. In order to decide whether it does happen always, we must turn to the concepts that form the subject-matter of the traditional philosophical sciences, and see whether an overlap of classes is a regular feature of their logical structure.

7. Logic distinguishes within the genus thought two species, judgement or proposition and inference. These, as subject-matter of separate parts of logical treatises, seem at first sight to be related much as the triangle and the circle are related in elementary geometry; and in that case they would, like the triangle and the circle, be mutually exclusive classes. But they are not mutually exclusive. That it is raining is a judgement; that it is raining because I can hear it is an inference. Of these two statements one includes the other; and it is therefore clear that the specific classes overlap: a judgement may also be an inference, an inference may also be a judgement.

'It is true,' I may be told, 'that judgement and inference are not mutually exclusive like triangle and circle; but this only shows that you were wrong to think of them as two species of thought. An inference is a complex structure built up out of a number of judgements in certain relations; if you want a geometrical analogy, think of judgement as a line and inference as a triangle.' I should welcome this criticism as an admission that, if species must exclude one another, judgement and inference cannot be species of a genus thought; but I should think the critic more courageous than wise; for his readiness to throw overboard the whole conception of genus and species, at the first hint of trouble, will lead him into difficulties whose magnitude I shrink from exploring at this point. The question will have to be considered later. In the meantime, there is another criticism to answer.

'You are first misapplying the rules of classification,' I may be told, 'and then blaming not yourself but them for the consequences. Instead of treating thought as a genus and dividing it into the species judgement and inference, you ought to have identified thought with judgement, and divided this into inferential and non-inferential or immediate.' But this would be a mere subterfuge; for the second of the two species is really nothing but judgement as such, and therefore identical with the genus; so that the ill consequences of making judgement and inference co-ordinate species of a genus are not avoided; there is only added the additional illogicality of identifying this genus with one of its own species.

The same difficulty reappears at the next stage in the classification. Within the judgement or proposition, logic distinguishes two species, affirmative and negative. According to the theory of classification it ought to be possible first to define the generic nature of judgement, without reference to its species, as we define the triangle without reference to the distinction between equilateral, isosceles, and scalene, and then to add the differentias of the two species separately. But if we try to define the judgement generically, we find that it cannot be done: either our attempt results in giving a definition of one species (the affirmative) for that of the genus, as when we say that a judgement affirms a predicate of a subject, or else it results in merely enumerating the species, as when we say that a judgement is that which either affirms or denies a predicate.

Nor is this the only difficulty at this stage. According to the theory of classification, affirmative and negative judgements ought to be two alternative species, each completely exhibiting the generic nature of judgement, as straight lines and curved lines each completely exhibit the generic nature of a line. But if, in the attempt to discover what exactly a negative judgement is, we take an example and purge it of everything affirmative, no student of logic needs to be reminded that we end by reducing it to nothing at all. At the moment when it becomes merely negative it ceases to be a significant judgement.

If that is so—and it is, as I say, a commonplace of the logical text-books—affirmative and negative judgements are so far from being mutually exclusive species that all negative judgements, and not some only, are also affirmative. But if the reader hesitates to accept this view, he will perhaps at least admit that there are some judgements which are at once affirmative and negative. If I say that my watch has stopped, I both affirm that its mechanism is at rest and deny that it is in motion; but this is not a compound statement made up of one affirmative and one negative proposition; I am making one statement, not two, and that statement is both the affirmation of one thing and the denial of its opposite.

The same liability to overlap may be seen in the other divisions of the judgement. The singular judgement, for syllogistic purposes, is regarded as a universal; and in fact it does combine universal and particular elements. The disjunctive is both categorical and hypothetical. And as for modality, a state of things which is not possible cannot be actual, nor can it very well help being actual if it is necessary. So also in the classification of inferences. Aristotle gives us an inductive syllogism; Mill a deductive method of induction.

Taking the classifications of traditional logic as they stand, therefore, it would appear that wherever we divide a genus into species, these species, instead of excluding each other like those of a scientific genus, overlap; or at any rate that this is the view of their relation which has always been held by traditional logic itself.

The critic whose observations I left unanswered

a few pages back may now claim a further hearing. He may insist: 'You have drawn the wrong inference. Such distinctions as you are describing, though they may have been called specifications of genera, are not really that; you have yourself proved that they cannot be, because they overlap. You have proved, rather, that affirmative and negative, universal and particular, and the like are elements co-existing in a single judgement like convex and concave in a single curve; but convex and concave are not kinds of curve, they are elements in an indivisible whole.'

To this I reply: you are right, if terms like species or kind must never be used except as they are used in connexion with the scientific concept. But is there any reason so to restrict them? Surely common sense allows us to speak of poetry and music as kinds of art, or induction and deduction as kinds of argument, with as good a conscience as when we call a circle and an ellipse two kinds of curve, or a bird and a fish two kinds of animal; although we are quite aware that those kinds overlap. And therefore I propose to go on using the word. Even if I gave it up, that would make no difference to the thing: namely, a peculiar type of logical structure found in philosophical concepts, which in some ways resembles the specification of a non-philosophical concept, but differs from it in that the species, elements, moments, or whatever you choose to call them, are exemplified in overlapping classes instead of mutually exclusive classes.

The critic shakes his head. 'You are pursuing a chimera,' I can hear him say. 'There is only one kind of logical structure possible to a concept: that in which the rules of classification are rigidly observed. Break them, and you have left the high road of logical thought to lose yourself among morasses. If traditional logic flouts these rules, so much the worse, not for them, but for it; and our duty is not to imitate it, but to reform it.' I shall return to this warning in the sequel; for the moment, I pass on to the case of ethics.

8. In ethics also, the traditionally recognized concepts are specified into overlapping classes. Take, for example, two such concepts: that of goods and that of actions.

Goods are traditionally divided into three species, *iucundum*, *utile*, *honestum*: let us call them the pleasant, the expedient, and the right. Some philosophers have denied that the pleasant is a kind of good, and others have said the same of the right; until the reasons of these denials have been considered, which shall be done by implication in the next chapter, I will leave them on one side and merely ask what those philosophers have meant who have said, as most have said, that these are kinds of good.

Clearly, no one has ever meant that they are mutually exclusive kinds. This would have implied that whatever is pleasant must therefore be both inexpedient and wrong; that whatever is expedient must be both wrong and unpleasant; and that whatever is right must be both unpleasant and inexpedient. And this, I imagine, no one has ever believed. Certainly it has not been a belief widely held among philosophers; for no one believing it could for a moment suppose either that virtue and happiness are the same, or that a man could enjoy doing his duty, or that actions are right in so far as they tend to promote happiness, or that pleasure is the sole good, or that virtue is the sole good. In a word, there is hardly any ethical theory, of all those that have been propounded, which could even be contemplated as possible by a person who denied the overlap of these three classes.

Actions are commonly divided into classes according as they are done from motives of different kinds: desire, self-interest, duty. The distinction is important because, according to the view commonly held, the moral value of an act differs according to the motive from which it is done, acts done from a motive of duty being morally good acts, and so forth. If it could be held that acts done from these different motives fall into separate and mutually exclusive classes, this would greatly ease the task of assigning to each act its true moral worth. But in spite of this temptation to believe the contrary, moral philosophers have always recognized that in fact our motives are often mixed, so that one and the same act may fall into two or even into all three classes.

These and similar considerations make it clear that in our ordinary thought about moral questions, whether we call this thought philosophy or common sense, we habitually think in terms of concepts whose specific classes, instead of excluding one another, overlap. For the present I am only concerned to establish this as a matter of fact: that we do think in this way, not that we are right to think in this way. The facts upon which I am insisting may appear to my critic an open scandal; to assert them may seem equivalent to admitting that our ordinary common-sense thought on moral questions is a perfect Augean stable of illogicality, and that what passes by the name of moral philosophy is no better; to insist on them, therefore, may seem only to support the programme of those who would banish ethical subjects from philosophy altogether, or else submit them to a ruthless purge by turning upon them a flood of logical cold water. At present, my only answer must be a plea for patience. The facts are far worse, from their point of view, than these reformers recognize. The scandal not only affects ethics, but, as we have seen, it affects logic too, and indeed all the other philosophical sciences. We must wait until we have ascertained the extent of the evil before we bring forward proposals for curing it.

9. The same overlap reappears in the relation between logic and ethics as two wholes. Thought and action, each considered in its essence, may be as distinct as we will; but in their existence in concrete instances they are so connected that it is possible, and more than possible, for an instance of the one to be an instance of the other also. Actual thinking is a labour to which ethical predicates may attach; and although it is a mistake to regard these

predicates as throwing any light on its nature as thinking—a mistake made by those who regard thought as essentially practical—they do throw light on the question under what conditions thought can exist. In the same way, although action itself is not thought, an instance of action may be an instance of thought also, and hence, without any confusion between the two essences, it is possible to speak of acting rationally, just as it is possible to speak of thinking resolutely.

It would be wearisome to pursue the same conception through metaphysics, aesthetics, and whatever other philosophical sciences are recognized. The reader can do it for himself; he will find that everywhere the same rule holds good, that the traditional specifications of philosophical concepts form overlapping classes. If for this reason he thinks that the traditional concepts, not only now in ethics, but throughout the field of philosophy, are riddled with contradictions, and must be revised with extreme rigour so as to make them conform to the rules of classification, let him attempt to revise them; if he does so he will find that they stubbornly resist his efforts, and that if he is too deeply attached to the rules of classification to countenance any thinking in which they are not observed, he must give up thinking at all about the topics which go by the name of philosophy. For this type of structure, in which specific classes overlap, is so deeply rooted in the subject-matters with which philosophy has always been concerned, that to set one's face against it means abjuring any attempt to think seriously about matters of that kind.

At this point, therefore, the reader is confronted with a choice. If he is satisfied that the traditional rules of classification must be rigidly applied to every concept whatever, and that to think of the specific classes of a genus as overlapping can only have fatal results for the whole structure of thought, he should read no farther in this essay. But if he is prepared to admit, I do not say that he understands how such an overlap is possible, but that philosophers may conceivably have been right so consistently to affirm it in spite of their own logical rules, then I invite him to join with me in the following experiment.

Let us assume that traditional philosophy in general is neither a body of truths to be blindly accepted nor a mass of errors to be repudiated wholesale, but a mixture of good things and bad; and in particular let us assume that on this question it has not been wholly at fault, but that in some sense, to be better discovered hereafter, an overlap of classes is characteristic of the philosophical concept, and may serve to distinguish it from those of exact and empirical science. Let us see where this assumption leads us. If by working it out we arrive at an account of philosophical method which is both consistent with itself and consonant with our experience of philosophical thinking, we shall be obliged to ask whether, after all, it is not more than a mere assumption. If it is merely a wanton defiance of logic, we can be sure of soon discovering the fact;

for logic is well able to revenge itself on those who defy it.

§ 3

10. From the assumption that the philosophical concept has a peculiar type of logical structure in which specific classes overlap, there is one negative inference which can be stated without delay. No method can be used in philosophy which depends for its validity on their mutual exclusion.

Such methods are often and rightly used in science. In all empirical sciences we collect instances of a generic concept and sort them into classes each presenting that concept in a specific form. This is the way in which we proceed as a matter of course when we wish to study the specifications of an empirical concept, for example the varieties of wild rose. The same method is applicable in exact science, but not so useful, because there the generic concept can be divided into its species *a priori*, without the trouble of sorting instances. In many sciences these two methods of dividing a concept are combined.

Suppose this method were applied in philosophy. Suppose, in order to study the specific forms of the generic concept action, we began by collecting individual instances of action, and then sorted them into actions done from duty, actions done from interest, and actions done from inclination; hoping, when this was finished, to examine each class in turn and so determine what features are common to all the actions in one class and absent from every action in the other two. Before long, we should find ourselves confronted by an overlap: certain actions, those in which motives were mixed, cannot be unambiguously assigned to any one class. What are we to do?

11. The right course would be to treat the overlap as a danger-signal: to stop using this method altogether, pending a careful inquiry as to its appropriateness. But there is always a temptation to ignore such warnings; and in this case yielding to the temptation will involve disqualifying the ambiguous instances, ruling them out of consideration because they will not fit into our scheme—whereas this is the very reason why we ought to attend more carefully to them—and confining our attention to that part of our subject-matter in which the overlap seems to be absent: actions in which we can persuade ourselves that the motives were absolutely unmixed.

The result will be that our theory as to the nature of any specific form of a generic concept will be built upon the margin where the overlap between this form and another has not yet made itself felt. This method of investigation is often followed. One philosopher, discussing the theory of perception and distinguishing veridical perception from illusion, will rule out of consideration all instances in which a perception seems tainted with the character of illusion, and will endeavour to study instances of purely and simply veridical perception. Another, studying the generic concept of goods and its specific form, that of things good in themselves, will propose as a method the question whether this or that thing would be good if nothing else existed, as if things good in themselves formed a separate class of goods, which would remain when everything possessed of a merely relative goodness had been thrown aside.

All such inquiries are vitiated by a fallacy, which may be called the fallacy of precarious margins. It consists in assuming that the overlap which has already affected a certain area of the class in question can be trusted not to spread, and that beyond its limit there lies a marginal region in which the instances exhibit only one of the specific forms, uncontaminated by the presence of the other. This margin is necessarily precarious, because once the overlap is admitted in principle there is no ground for assuming that it will stop at any particular point; and the only sound canon of method is so to conduct the inquiry that its results would stand firm however far the overlap extended.

12. But it is possible to avoid this fallacy at the cost of falling into another. Once it is recognized that the overlap is in principle unlimited, and that sound method requires him to proceed as if the two specific classes coincided throughout their extension, a philosopher who has begun by thinking that every concept must have a group of instances to itself may conclude that, since there is only one group of instances, there is only one concept: he therefore declares his two specific concepts identical. Thus, it is observed that a man who does his duty often thereby increases the happiness of people in general;

it is reasonably conjectured that this is so, not often merely, but always; and it is concluded that since a dutiful action always increases the general happiness, there is no distinction between the concept of duty and the concept of promoting happiness. Errors of this type are so common that a catalogue of them might fill a book. The false principle at work in them is that, where there is no difference in the extension of two concepts, there is no distinction between the concepts themselves. This I propose to call the fallacy of identified coincidents.

13. These two fallacies are alternative applications of a single principle which, however true in exact and empirical science, is false in philosophy: the principle that when a generic concept is divided into its species there is a corresponding division of its instances into mutually exclusive classes. I call this the fallacy of false disjunction, because it consists in the disjunctive proposition that any instance of a generic concept must fall either in one or in another of its specific classes; and this is false because, since they overlap, it may fall in both. Applied positively, this yields the fallacy of precarious margins: namely that, since there admittedly is a distinction between two concepts, there must be a difference between their instances. Applied negatively, it yields the fallacy of identified coincidents: namely that, since the instances can admittedly not be separated, there is no distinguishing the concepts.

14. The first rule of philosophical method, then, will be to beware of false disjunctions and to assume

that the specific classes of a philosophical concept are always liable to overlap, so that two or more specifically differing concepts may be exemplified in the same instances. A useful reminder of this rule is Aristotle's formula for the overlap of classes: he is in the habit of saying about two concepts *ἔστι μὲν τὸ αὐτὸ τὸ δὲ εἶναι αὐτοῖς οὐ τὸ αὐτό*: the two concepts 'are the same thing' in the sense that a thing which exemplifies the one exemplifies the other also, but 'their being is not the same' in the sense that being an instance of the one is not the same as being an instance of the other. The traditional way of referring to this principle is to speak of 'a distinction without a difference', that is, a distinction in the concepts without a difference in the instances. The rule may be put, then, by saying that any distinction in philosophy may be a distinction without a difference; or, alternatively, that where two philosophical concepts are distinguished Aristotle's formula may hold good, that the two are the same thing but their being is different.

15. It may be of interest, at the conclusion of this chapter, to glance forward and ask how the observance of this rule will affect a philosopher's expectations of the direction in which his thought is likely to move and the results which it is likely to achieve; although at this stage any such anticipations will be merely negative, being too vague and general for positive statement.

A philosophy proceeding according to this rule cannot set before itself as an end the classification of its subject-matter, as a botanist or naturalist may regard it as an end to distinguish and arrange species of plants or animals. For the subject-matter of philosophy, owing to the overlap of its classes, does not admit of classification in that sense. It can be classified only in a provisional and temporary manner, such classification being therefore not an end in itself but only a means to the distinguishing of elements which coexist in actual fact: thus we may classify actions into those done from duty and those done from inclination, so long as we remember that our instances of each are almost sure to be instances of the other as well, and use the classification merely as a means to fixing our attention on the specific peculiarities of acting from duty as such and acting from inclination as such. The true work of philosophy will be the distinguishing of concepts like these, coexisting in their instances.

16. But distinguishing such concepts cannot mean simply enumerating the various elements which analysis can detect coexisting in a concrete fact. For these elements will be specifications of a single concept, and therefore there will be logical relations between them; to represent the fact as a mere aggregate of elements coexisting without any such logical bonds will be to leave an essential part of the analytic work undone. In an empirical concept like man, there is no apparent connexion between such elements as having ten toes and having the power of speech; but in a philosophical concept there cannot be this looseness of structure,

and the various elements must be somehow interrelated. Hence no object of philosophical thought can be rightly conceived as a mere aggregate, whether of logically distinguished elements or of spatial or temporal parts; the parts or elements, however proper it may be to distinguish them, cannot be conceived as separable; and therefore it is impossible that such an object should be either put together out of parts or elements separately pre-existing, or divided into parts or elements which can survive the division; for either of these would imply that the connexions between the parts are accidental, whereas they must in reality be essential.

17. Here a reader may say: 'By extracting these consequences from a simple rule of method, you are committing yourself to metaphysical statements of a far-reaching and highly disputable kind, where you cannot expect your readers to follow you.' But this would be to misunderstand my purpose. A principle of method is necessarily provisional. To commit oneself to it at the beginning of one's inquiries, as a cast-iron rule to be followed, come what may, in every possible variety of problem and subject-matter, would be foreign to the whole spirit of philosophical thinking. Thinking philosophically, whatever else it means, means constantly revising one's starting-point in the light of one's conclusions and never allowing oneself to be controlled by any cast-iron rule whatever. What I have done is merely to issue a warning against two unadvised assumptions: first, that the object of which philosophy is in search will

turn out to be a classificatory system; secondly, that this object will turn out to be an aggregate of parts. And I do not even say that one or other of these assumptions may not eventually prove correct; only that neither can eventually prove correct if, as seems to be the case at this stage of our inquiry, the philosophical concept really has a peculiar logical structure in which specific classes overlap. A person who begins a philosophical inquiry with the assumption that the object of which he is in search has the structure either of a classificatory system or of an aggregate of parts, is committing himself to the assumption that this apparent overlap of classes is an illusion. For my part, I am pursuing the hypothesis that it is not an illusion; and on that hypothesis any philosophy which aims at conceiving its object as a classificatory system or an aggregate of parts is misconceiving its own aims and therefore its own nature and methods.

III
THE SCALE OF FORMS

§ 1

THE philosophical concept has been hitherto discussed as if, apart from the overlap of its specific classes, it resembled other concepts in structure. But if this overlap is real it cannot be an isolated peculiarity. The differences between the species of a non-philosophical concept are of such a kind that an overlap between them is unthinkable; of what kind, then, must be the differences between the species of a philosophical concept, that an overlap between them should be possible?

1. We distinguish differences of degree from differences of kind. A beginning may be made by asking if either of these, taken separately, would explain the overlap.

It is not explained by a mere difference of degree. If all instances of a generic concept had one and the same attribute in varying degrees, and if the genus were divided into species according to these variations, there could be no overlap; for the point at which any one specific class began would be the point at which another ended. Examples are the classification of books for a librarian's purpose by size, and the classification of men by age for military service.

It seems in fact to be generally admitted that no philosophical importance attaches to mere differences of degree. Philosophers are often engaged with the question whether a certain thing possesses a certain attribute or not; whether, for instance, a bad work of art possesses some beauty or none at all; but the mere degree to which the attribute is present is held as a rule to be a matter outside their province. Indeed, some of them hold that the attributes in which they are especially interested, such as beauty, goodness, truth, reality, admit of no degrees; and others, who would prefer to recognize degrees in such matters, do not think that these by themselves and apart from all differences in kind serve as basis for the logical division of the concepts; they think rather of the differences in degree as somehow connected with differences in kind, so that the concept is specified not according to mere differences of degree, but according to some combination of differences in degree with differences in kind.

2. Mere differences in kind are equally impotent to explain an overlap of classes. Non-philosophical concepts, such as that of a conic section, may be specified in this way, as into ellipse, parabola, hyperbola, and so forth; but this type of specification cannot yield overlapping classes; the ellipse passes into a parabola when one focus is removed to infinity, but this does not imply an overlap.

This again is generally recognized. The concept of sensation, for example, is one with which philosophers have been much concerned; but when the genus sensation is divided into the species seeing, hearing, smelling, and so forth, differentiated solely by kind, philosophers leave the separate consideration of these separate species to psychologists and physiologists. As specified purely on a basis of kind, therefore, sensation is regarded as a non-philosophical concept, or rather as a concept in a non-philosophical phase.

3. Sometimes, however, differences of kind are found in combination with differences of degree; and in that case philosophers are more apt to take notice of them. If the distinctions between the various virtues, whether the cardinal virtues, temperance, fortitude, wisdom, and justice, or the theological, faith, hope, and charity, or those of any other scheme, are merely specific ways of behaving well or being well disposed, differing among themselves only in kind, philosophers in general would recognize that to insert a discussion of each into a theory of virtue would be to load the theory with empirical detail; but if, as Plato thought about the cardinal virtues and St. Paul about the theological, they differ among themselves also in degree, some being higher than others on a scale of some sort, most philosophers would feel, whether they could justify the feeling or no, that a discussion of them would be of genuinely philosophical interest. So for the various arts, painting, poetry, music, and the rest: if they are merely embodiments of the aesthetic spirit in different kinds of matter, a philosophy of art, as distinct from an empirical description of art, would prefer to ignore them; if they embody that

spirit in different degrees, as some have thought, they are generally recognized as belonging to its subject-matter.

It seems, then, that where differences of degree exist in combination with differences of kind philosophical thought is more interested in them than in either existing separately; and this gives a hint that some such combination may provide the answer to our question.

4. The combination of differences in degree with differences in kind implies that a generic concept is specified in a somewhat peculiar way. The species into which it is divided are so related that each not only embodies the generic essence in a specific manner, but also embodies some variable attribute in a specific degree. In respect of the variable, each specific form of the concept differs from the rest in degree; in respect of the manner in which the generic essence is specified, each differs from the rest in kind. In such a system of specifications the two sets of differences are so connected that whenever the variable, increasing or decreasing, reaches certain critical points on the scale, one specific form disappears and is replaced by another. A breaking strain, a freezing-point, a minimum taxable income, are examples of such critical points on a scale of degrees where a new specific form suddenly comes into being. A system of this kind I propose to call a scale of forms.

It is a conception with a long history in philosophical thought. It is a favourite with Plato, who has various scales or attempts at a scale of the forms of knowledge: nescience, opinion, knowledge; conjecture, opinion, understanding, reason; poetry, mathematics, dialectic; a scale of the forms of being, from nothing through half-being to true being; scales of the forms of pleasure, those of the body and those of the soul, the latter more truly pleasures than the former, or the impure and the pure, or a gradation from pain through quiescence to true pleasure; scales of the forms of political constitutions, and so on almost endlessly. What is significant in Plato is not so much the actual scale of forms by which in one or another passage he expounds the structure of this or that concept, as the evident conviction, pervading all his work, that this is the type of structure which philosophical concepts possess.

Nor is it a conviction peculiar to Plato, together with the neo-Platonists, the Christian mystics, the Platonists of the Renaissance, and others who may be suspected of drinking more deeply than wisely at the river of Platonic thought. Aristotle recognizes the same type of logical structure, for example when he distinguishes the vegetable, animal, and human 'souls' as three forms of life arranged on a scale so that each includes its predecessor and adds to it something new. Locke classifies his main types of knowledge explicitly into 'degrees'. Leibniz attempted to make of it a central principle of philosophical method, as the law of continuity. Kant, whether through the influence of Leibniz or *rebus ipsis dictantibus*, reverts to it again and again, even at the cost of apparent or real inconsistency, as in the doctrine of the schematism of the categories, where imagination becomes an intermediary between sense and understanding, with a world of its own which is a kind of Platonic *μίμημα* of the world of understanding. The positivists and evolutionists of the nineteenth century were no less emphatic in their belief that knowledge was specified into grades on a scale of abstraction, and nature into specific forms on a scale of development. In short, attempts to use the double criterion of degree and kind as a key to the structure of the philosophical concept have been so universal that it is hardly possible to study the history of thought without suspecting their correspondence with some permanent characteristic of those concepts.

5. This type of structure, however, is not peculiar to philosophical concepts. Ice, water, and steam make up a scale of forms; they differ from each other both in degree, as hotter or colder, and in kind, as specifically different states of the same body. Scientific thought is familiar with such cases: the periodic table of the elements, the specific differences between youth, maturity, and old age, and so forth.

But there seems to be a difference between a philosophical and a non-philosophical scale of forms in one important respect. In a non-philosophical scale, the variable is something extraneous to the generic essence: thus the essence of water, that which is common to its solid, liquid, and gaseous forms, is represented by the formula H_2O, and heat does not appear in this formula either explicitly or by implication. Hence, however widely the degree of heat varies, the generic essence of water remains unchanged. Not only are all three forms equally forms of water, each fully entitled to that name and all that it implies, but even if the variable vanished altogether and the temperature fell to absolute zero the substance which had reached that temperature would still be H_2O.

6. In a philosophical scale of forms, the variable is identical with the generic essence itself. In Plato's scales of the forms of knowledge, the variable is given as 'definiteness' or 'truth' (σαφήνεια, ἀλήθεια) which are essential characteristics of knowledge; in his scale of being, it is reality; and the specific object of opinion, in so far as it is unfit to be an object for anything higher, is so because it is not wholly real and is characterized by a certain indeterminacy of being which is related to real being as confusion of mind is related to real thought; in his scale of political forms, only the highest truly deserves the name political, the rest are in varying degrees non-political; and so on for the others.

In this, once more, Plato is not singular. For Leibniz, the forms of knowledge are differentiated by their degrees of 'clearness and distinctness'; but here, as with Plato, the variable belongs to the essence of knowledge itself; in calling sensation 'confused conception' Leibniz is calling it knowledge —for, on his view, all knowledge is conception—but qualifying that statement by an epithet indicating that it is knowledge only in a low degree. Of Locke's 'degrees of knowledge' the highest, intuition, is alone wholly knowledge; the lowest, judgement, 'never amounts to knowledge, no not to that which is the lowest degree of it'; and the middle, demonstration, is intermediate in degree, showing as it does 'some sparks of bright knowledge'. The exact correspondence in point of structure between this scale and the Platonic scales of being or pleasure is especially instructive in a philosopher who can hardly be accused of Platonizing tendencies.

These instances are perhaps enough to convince the reader, if he needs conviction, that there are some grounds for saying that where we find expositions of a philosophical as opposed to a non-philosophical scale of forms we find the variable identified with the generic essence. The result of this identification is that every form, so far as it is low in the scale, is to that extent an imperfect or inadequate specification of the generic essence, which is realized with progressive adequacy as the scale is ascended.

§ 2

7. The idea of a philosophical scale of forms has been stated in the foregoing pages merely as one that has repeatedly appeared in the history of thought. It remains to ask whether the many philosophers who have used this idea as a key to the structure of the philosophical concept have been right so to use it. The first step towards answering this question must be to raise certain obvious difficulties.

The idea of a scale of forms is easy enough to accept when the generic essence is one thing and the variable another; for in that case each specific form is completely and equally with all the others an embodiment of the generic essence, and therefore a real species of that genus. But if the variable and the generic essence are the same, the idea contains an element of paradox; for the lower forms on the scale are not, except in a relatively low degree, species of the genus at all; and since it seems obvious that a given concept must either be or not be a species of a given genus, and that this is not a relation admitting of degrees, it seems impossible to evade the dilemma that either these lower forms are species of the genus, in which case they are completely species of it, or that they are not completely species of it, in which case they are not species of it to any degree whatever. In either case the idea of a scale of forms whose variable is identical with the generic essence falls to the ground, condemned as a tissue of contradictions, a logician's nightmare.

There are criticisms which, merely because they are so obvious, cannot be admitted without misgiving. This is one which is so well within the powers of any beginner, after reading the first few chapters of a logical text-book, that the question irresistibly suggests itself: which is the more likely, that Plato and Aristotle and Leibniz and Locke, and the other philosophers who have used the idea, all by some curious coincidence made the same elementary blunder, or that the criticism rests on a misunderstanding? And if this answer fails to impress the critic, let him reflect that his criticism proceeds from the assumption that the doctrines concerning the structure of the concept, which are expressed in elementary text-books of logic, must be accepted without question and applied without modification as principles of philosophical method; whereas the assumption which in the last chapter we agreed to make, was that in their application to philosophy they may require some modification. Under the terms of our compact, therefore, this criticism should strictly be ruled out of order; for the time being we may postpone it until we have considered a second and more urgent difficulty.

8. This is the question whether the idea of a scale of forms, as hitherto stated, serves to explain the overlap between the species of a philosophical genus. The answer is yes, if these species are opposites: no, if they are distincts. If actions, for example, are divided into the opposite species good and bad, these terms in themselves will be the infinity and zero ends of a scale of forms, and the intermediate forms will partake of both opposites, each being good to a certain degree, and also bad to a certain degree in so far as it is not better; so that in all intermediate cases there will be an overlap of goodness and badness, and the only cases left in the margins outside the overlap will be the pure abstractions of goodness and badness in themselves, if indeed these are conceivable. The intermediates, on the contrary, being determined each by a unique combination of

the extremes, must be mutually exclusive : where one begins, the next ends.

In an overlap or coincidence of opposites there is nothing paradoxical and nothing peculiar to philosophy. Water, at any given temperature, is hot in so far as it attains that temperature, and cold in so far as it attains only that; wherever there is a scale of degrees there is a coexistence of opposites at every point in the scale. But in this special case of a philosophical concept the overlap of opposites has a curious result.

9. A concept may be specified either by opposition, as actions are divided into good and bad, or by distinction, as actions are divided into just, generous, courageous, and so forth. If overlapping, as we assumed in the preceding chapter, is characteristic of philosophical species, and if opposites overlap while distincts do not, philosophical species are always opposites and never distincts. Hence in a scale of forms the extremes, being related by opposition, are philosophical species of the generic concept; the intermediates, being related by distinction, are non-philosophical. Opposite species like good and bad will thus belong to the philosophical phase of their genus, and will provide appropriate subject-matter for philosophical thought; distinct species like just, generous, and courageous will belong to its non-philosophical phase, and must be banished from philosophy to some other sphere of thought.

This leads to a simple and straightforward rule

of philosophical method: since philosophical specification is into opposites and non-philosophical into distincts, any distinctions found in a philosophical subject-matter must be either banished from it as alien to the sphere of philosophy or else interpreted so as to appear cases of opposition. It is not enough to show that these distinctions contain in themselves an element or aspect of opposition; that will not save them; the element of distinction must be completely eliminated and nothing except pure opposition allowed to remain.

10. Certain consequences of this rule can be easily foreseen. First, the embarrassing idea of a scale of forms in which the variable is identical with the generic essence can be dispensed with; for in such a scale the intermediates are eliminated and only the extremes are left; and thus all those connecting links which philosophers have from time to time interpolated between opposites can and must be struck out, not merely as unnecessary complications but as positive errors. Those ambiguous twilight third terms which appear in the Platonic scales—the spirited element between reason and appetite in the soul; the quiescence between pleasure and pain; the limbo where things welter between being and nothingness—the imagination that connects sense and understanding in Kant's schematism—and so on, down to all the monstrous concatenations of the Hegelian dialectic—all this can be simplified away until each philosophical concept stands stripped and bare as a genus specified into pure opposites whose

inversely varying degrees of realization differ among themselves merely empirically.

11. Secondly, the same rule will apply to the relation between any one philosophical concept and any other. When all distinction is gone, the distinction between these cannot remain; there is no longer one philosophical problem or group of problems in logic, one in ethics, and so forth, for the characteristics that mark off each of these from the rest are examples of distinction and therefore extraneous to philosophy; and nothing is left except a single pair of opposites, the mere abstract idea of opposite terms, which have no particular nature and no particular name—for any names by which we may call them, such as the one and the many, subject and object, and the like, are borrowed from the non-philosophical realm of distinction—colliding eternally in a void.

The first consequence cannot fail to seem attractive. It amounts to this: that philosophy has taken power to jettison all distinctions as merely empirical, and is free to simplify itself at discretion by relegating to a non-philosophical sphere, labelled as history, science, or what not, all the conceptions with which it has no wish to deal, and to concentrate afresh on its cardinal problems. But the first consequence leads inevitably to the second. The same criterion which has begun by banishing encumbrances must go on to banish essentials. Point by point, the whole subject-matter of philosophy is thrown aside, and every problem is reduced to a mere empirical variant of one single problem, the problem of opposites, which is not a problem because it has been solved; and all its empirical variants can be solved, if that can be called solving them, by mechanically repeating the formula of this ready-made solution.

12. Even this may to some minds appear an attractive prospect, so let us proceed to a third consequence. The philosophical scale of forms has been disintegrated into a philosophical relation and a non-philosophical, the first between opposites, the second between distincts. But this same analysis will apply to a non-philosophical scale of forms. Here too there are opposites, heat and cold, and distincts, ice, water, and steam; if specification into opposites is the mark of the philosophical concept, heat and cold with their genus temperature are subject-matter for philosophy; and the theory of heat becomes a matter which the physicist must hand over to the philosopher, although he may keep as his own the specific differences between ice, water, and steam.

Neither can be expected to welcome this proposal; yet it cannot be rejected, if opposition is the principle of philosophical specification and distinction that of non-philosophical; and no one can reject it who wishes to confine the subject-matter of aesthetics, for example, to the opposition between beauty and ugliness, relegating all degrees and kinds of beauty to the rag-bag of empirical thought, or, logical consequence of this, to restrict the work of philosophy to the exposition of a single clash of opposites, endlessly repeated in endless historical avatars.

13. It may be thought a consequence alarming enough to persuade a reader that the argument has gone astray; but alarm is not the best motive for rejecting a philosophical argument; it would be better to hold our course until we are driven from it by some unanswerable reason. Let us consider, then, that the argument has brought us to a dilemma. Is the relation between philosophical specification by opposites and non-philosophical specification by distincts itself a case of distinction or of opposition? If distinction, then specification in general is a non-philosophical concept, since it is specified on the non-philosophical principle; and thus the attempt to maintain a dualism of philosophical and non-philosophical thought has ended by absorbing the conception of philosophical thought into a system of non-philosophical thought in which its own characteristics are necessarily lost. But if it is a case of opposition, every concept is in some degree philosophical and in some degree non-philosophical; the assigning of this or that particular concept to one or other category is impossible; philosophical logic as the logic of opposites has triumphed over non-philosophical logic as the logic of distincts, and with this triumph it has destroyed the distinction between itself and its opponent.

Thus if either horn of the dilemma is accepted the dualism of philosophical and non-philosophical thought breaks down by the absorption of one into the other; but the result is equally disastrous if an escape is made between the horns. If the relation between opposition and distinction is itself neither a mere opposition nor a mere distinction, but both at once, or (what comes to the same) some third thing intermediate between them, this very fact shows that the dualism was an error, since a third term has been found; and the question must be raised, whether philosophical specification is really by pure opposition, and not rather by this newly-discovered third principle.

This question must be further considered hereafter. For the present, the dilemma has brought the argument to a standstill. We have worked out a preliminary sketch of the idea of a scale of forms; it has led us deeper and deeper into a thicket of paradoxes, and at last to a place from which there is no forward road except at the cost of abandoning the presuppositions we have brought with us; and we had best go back to the beginning of our argument to find where the first false step was made.

§ 3

14. The preliminary idea of a scale of forms was arrived at by combining differences of degree with differences of kind. Going back to the beginning, therefore, means reconsidering the notions of these two types of difference. Philosophical specification, it was suggested, appears to combine them; but what are they before being combined? Is there any difference of meaning as between two usages of the term degree, in philosophy and elsewhere?

Differences of degree occur both in philosophical

and in non-philosophical concepts. We say that one man or action is better than another, and we say that one body is hotter than another. Now, as between these two examples, there is at least this difference: that the heat in a body can be measured whereas the goodness of a man or action cannot. Equally impossible it is to measure degrees of beauty, truth, pleasantness, or any other philosophical concept.

This is sometimes denied; but it would not, I think, be denied by any one who bore in mind the difference between measuring a thing and estimating its size without measurement. Looking at two books that are now before me, I estimate their relative height and say that one is twice as tall as the other; but this, which is precisely not measuring, is the most that any one thinks can be done for pleasures or goods. When I measure the books, I find that one is fifteen inches high and the other seven and a quarter; so that the ratio is not two to one, but two and a thirtieth to one. If some one tells me that this thing is twice as pleasant as that, but boggles at distinguishing between the presence or absence of the odd thirtieth, I know that he has not measured but has, at most, merely estimated; I say at most, because it is always possible that he is neither measuring nor estimating, but is using quantitative terms in order to express metaphorically something not itself quantitative.

The confessed inaccuracy of alleged measurements of goodness, pleasure, and the like is sometimes excused on the plea that all measurement is approximate. But the inaccuracy of genuine measurement is restricted within a known margin of error, which even in the crudest measurements is generally less than one per cent.; and up to this margin, for example in asserting that my larger book is within a tenth of an inch more or less than fifteen inches, our statements based on measurement are strictly accurate. Where these two conditions—known margin of error, and complete confidence in the accuracy of our figures up to that margin—are not satisfied, there is no measurement; and in the so-called measurements of pleasure, goodness, and so forth there is no attempt to satisfy them.

This objection is overcome only when, as happens in the psychological laboratory, genuine instrumental measuring replaces rough estimates of quantity. But in this case what is measured is not pleasure or the like, but certain bodily functions whose intensification roughly corresponds with an intensification of pleasure or whatever it may be. To say that pleasure admits of measurement by such means, therefore, is to confuse pleasure with these bodily concomitants of it.

15. In point of fact, then, we do not and cannot measure these differences; but it may still be held that the quantitative language sometimes applied to them, though it cannot represent measurements, may represent estimates of quantity rather than a metaphorical expression of something else; for, it may be argued, these things must be in principle measurable, on the ground that whatever exceeds

another thing must exceed it by a definite and therefore measurable amount.

I will waive the difficulty of understanding how degrees of pleasure can be measurable in principle but not in practice. I see how this can be said concerning the diameter of the sun, because to us it is inaccessible; but if a man can measure his own skull and not his own feelings, I should have thought it could only be because feelings as such resist measurement. But it is more important to point out that the alleged ground of this measurableness is open to criticism.

In heat as known to the physicist there are differences of degree; so there are in the heat we feel as a bodily sensation. In physical heat, the excess of one over another is a definite amount: we can raise a pint of water from one temperature to another by adding a certain amount of heat. In heat as we feel it, this is not the case. We cannot add a slightly tepid feeling to a feeling of moderate warmth and so produce a feeling of greater warmth. An intense feeling may be produced by a sum of small stimuli, each of which by itself would have produced a lesser feeling; but it is not itself a sum of these lesser feelings; where it exists, they do not exist at all.

As I move my hand nearer to the fire, I feel it grow hotter; but every increase in the heat I feel is also a change in the kind of feeling I experience; from a faint warmth through a decided warmth it passes to a definite heat, first pleasant, then dully painful, then sharply painful; the heat at one degree soothes me, at another excites me, at another torments me. I can detect as many differences in kind as I can detect differences in degree; and these are not two sets of differences but one single set. I can call them differences of degree if I like, but I am using the word in a special sense, a sense in which differences of degree not merely entail, but actually are, differences of kind.

This applies to all differences of degree among the specifications of a philosophical concept. They are never mere differences of degree with which can be connected a series of differences in kind; they are differences of a peculiar type, which are differences at once in degree and in kind. This is why they cannot be measured, for measurement applies only to pure differences of degree; and this is the real basis of the distinction between a philosophical scale of forms and a non-philosophical: in a non-philosophical scale there are differences of degree, and co-ordinated with them differences of kind; in a philosophical scale there is only one set of differences having this peculiar double character.

I call it peculiar, but it is a type of difference quite familiar to common sense, which here as elsewhere knows both the philosophical and the non-philosophical phase of the concept, and in speaking of degrees of kindred and affinity, the capital and other degrees of punishment, nobility and gentry and other degrees in the structure of society, university degrees, the degrees of comparison in grammar, and so forth, recognizes actual fusions of differences in degree, in the narrower or non-philosophical sense, with differences in kind.

16. That there must in a philosophical subject-matter be such a fusion, as distinct from any mere combination, of difference in degree with difference in kind, follows from the principle of overlapping classes. Differences in degree and differences in kind are two species of the genus difference, and in the case of philosophical concepts they must accordingly overlap to form a type of difference partaking of the nature of both. Instead of two types of difference, such as we find in the forms of water, one in degree of heat, which is measurable, the other in kind of physical structure, which gives rise to mutually exclusive specifications co-ordinated with the degrees of heat, it follows from our fundamental assumption that in the specification of a philosophical concept there must always be one single type of difference: a difference in degree, but not measurable, and a difference in kind, but not susceptible of arrangement in ungraded species; a difference, that is, between various forms in which the generic essence is embodied, which is also a difference in the degree to which these forms embody it.

17. Beside difference of degree and difference of kind, there is another pair of terms whose relation calls for thought before we can return to our main subject: opposition and distinction. Hitherto it has been assumed that concepts may be related either in one of these ways or in the other, and we have tried in vain to base on this assumption an account

of the difference between philosophical and non-philosophical specification; we must therefore reconsider the assumption.

In its non-philosophical phase, opposition is a relation subsisting between a positive term and its own mere negation or absence. Cold, as understood by the physicist, is the lack of heat; it is nothing but a name for the fact that in any given body there is not more heat present; at the zero end of the scale, it is a name for the fact that there is no heat present at all. But cold as we feel it is not mere lack of heat as we feel it, but another feeling with a positive character of its own; yet these are not two distinct feelings merely, but two opposite feelings. The relation of physical cold to the physical heat of which it is the negation I call pure or mere opposition; the relation of felt cold to felt heat is at once opposition and distinction, these two being fused into a single relation.

The same is true of the relation between good and bad. To call a man bad is not merely to say that he does fewer good acts, or acts less good in their degree or kind, than another whom we call good; it is to say that he does acts positively bad. What is bad is thus distinct from what is good as well as opposed to it. And the same relation recurs as between truth and error, beauty and ugliness, and all the pairs of opposites that figure in philosophical thought. Thus in general the kind of opposition which is found among philosophical terms is at once opposition and distinction, and subsists between terms each having a definite character of its own and yet forming together a true pair of opposites.

18. This again could have been predicted by considering the consequences of our original assumption. Distinction and opposition are two species of relation; and where the term relation is applied to a philosophical subject-matter it acquires the special colouring proper to philosophical concepts, that is, on our assumption, it denotes a generic concept whose specific classes overlap. In philosophical thought, therefore, distinction and opposition will necessarily combine into a peculiar type of relation which is neither mere distinction nor mere opposition, but partakes of both these characters; a relation which subsists between terms at once opposed and distinct.

19. To sum up. Differences of degree and differences of kind, which in non-philosophical thought can be disentangled from one another, are in philosophy fused into a new type of difference uniting the characteristics of both. Distinction and opposition, which in non-philosophical thought are two mutually exclusive kinds of relation, in philosophy coalesce into one, so that what seems at first sight a mere opposition—the relation, that is, between a term and its own absence—turns out to be also a distinction between two terms, and vice versa.

With these considerations in mind, we must go back to the conception of a scale of forms, reinterpret it, and ask whether as so reinterpreted it can overcome the first of the two defects which we found in our original sketch of the conception: namely, that it implied that the species of a genus can embody the generic essence in varying degrees, whereas it seems self-evident that any one specific form must embody the generic essence completely.

§ 4

20. If in philosophical thought every difference of kind is also a difference of degree, the specifications of a philosophical concept are bound to form a scale; and in this scale their common essence is bound to be realized differentially in degree as well as differentially in kind. The identification of the variable with the generic essence is thus no confusion, but a necessary consequence of the special characteristics of philosophical thought.

When from this point of view we look back at a few examples of philosophical scales of forms, we shall perhaps recognize that the identification of the variable with the generic essence loses all appearance of paradox in the light of this fusion of differences in degree with differences in kind; and it becomes plain that this appearance arose from forcing upon the facts of philosophical thinking an interpretation in which the terms difference of degree and difference of kind bore the special meanings proper to them in a non-philosophical context.

21. Where one work of art is more beautiful than another, no great subtlety of thought is needed to recognize that it is beautiful in a different way; it does not merely exceed the other, for the other has

its own kind of beauty, and can only be beaten by one which achieves a beauty of a higher kind. Thus it is not wholly true that there are degrees of beauty, if this means that beauty differs from beauty not in kind but only in degree; nor is it true that there are no such degrees, if this means that the kinds of beauty are all perfect each in its own way; for they are different in degree as well as in kind, so that the beauty of a comic epigram, however perfect, is not only the beauty of a small thing compared with the *Iliad*, but is a lesser as well as a different beauty.

The same is true of pleasure, goodness, and the other concepts belonging to the sphere of philosophy. Hastily considered, they may seem to obey the traditional rules of specification, modified by an overlap of classes; more closely scrutinized, they always reveal this characteristic fusion of differences in degree with differences in kind.

22. When attempts are made not merely to differentiate classes of good things but to distinguish kinds of goodness, it is constantly found that some of these kinds are more truly goodness than others. Thus if virtue, knowledge, and pleasure are taken as three things each having its own kind of goodness, it seems clear that pleasure, however intense and however lasting, belongs to an inferior order of goods as compared with virtue; inferior, that is, in goodness.[1] A similar result follows when the con-

[1] Cf. Ross, *The Right and the Good*, vi. It is there argued that virtue is a higher kind of good than knowledge, and knowledge than pleasure; these three species, with their differences of kind

cept of goodness is divided in other ways; for example if things good in themselves are distinguished from things relatively good, or actions having moral goodness from actions having the goodness of expediency. It seems impossible to recognize a genuine difference of kind in goodness without recognizing that in these kinds goodness is present in varying degrees.

23. Pleasure is one kind of good, but by common consent a relatively low kind. For this reason some have scrupled to think of it as good at all; but these scruples may be neglected when the idea of a scale of forms has been grasped. The concept of pleasure is not only one specific form in such a scale; it is itself, as a genus, specified in the same manner. Different pleasures are not only, as Bentham thought, different in duration and intensity (his other 'dimensions' may be ignored, as referring to something other than the intrinsic value of this or that pleasure); they differ also, as John Stuart Mill pointed out, in 'quality'; and by this he did not mean moral goodness or some other quality distinct from pleasantness, he meant quality 'merely as a pleasure', that is, pleasantness itself, as a thing admitting differences at once of degree and of kind. It was by the criterion of pleasure that Mill thought it better to be Socrates dissatisfied than a fool satisfied; the pleasures of Socrates, even if inferior to the fool's by Bentham's quantitative tests, are superior in quality, so that they

fused with differences of degree so that the latter are not measurable, making up what I call a scale of forms.

deserve the name of pleasure in a sense in which the fool's do not. Mill is in fact asserting that pleasures form a scale in which the higher are more pleasant than the lower; and this is none the less true for being, though Mill overlooked the fact, fatal to the project of a hedonistic calculus.

24. The conception of a type of difference which is at once a difference in degree and a difference in kind releases philosophical thought from a series of errors which fall into two groups.

Because it is recognized that there are differences of degree in the subject-matter of philosophy, it is sometimes assumed that these resemble the differences of degree found in a non-philosophical concept like the physicist's heat: that is, that they are differences of degree pure and simple, and therefore susceptible of measurement and calculation. From this fallacy arise all the attempts to treat philosophical matters like pleasures, goods, and so forth mathematically; attempts so uniformly unsuccessful that no one, perhaps, would be tempted to make them but for the fear of falling into the opposite error. This is the fallacy of assuming that, because the species of a philosophical genus differ in kind, they exhibit no differences of degree; from which it would follow that all pleasures were equally pleasant, all good things or good acts equally good, all beautiful things equally beautiful, and so forth. These may be called the fallacy of calculation and the fallacy of indifference respectively; they represent the two horns of a dilemma based on the false disjunction that a difference of degree cannot also be a difference of kind (false disjunction of degree and kind).

Here, as often happens with dilemmas, the victim may impale himself on both horns successively. First, by the fallacy of indifference, he may argue that pushpin is as good as poetry; then, redressing the balance by adopting the fallacy of calculation, he may try to represent those differences of degree which at first he ignored by a calculus in which one of these indifferent units is added to another.

§ 5

No less important are the modifications introduced into the idea of a scale of forms by the fusion of distinction with opposition.

25. In the provisional sketch of that idea, the scale was described as consisting of extremes, opposed to one another and representing the infinity and zero values of the variable, and intermediates, representing various degrees of their inverse combination. But if the variable is identical with the generic essence, the zero end forms no part of the scale; for in it the generic essence is altogether absent. The lower end of the scale, therefore, lies not at zero, but at unity, or the minimum realization of the generic essence.

This might seem to imply that, since the scale contains no absolute opposite to the generic essence, opposition as an element in the logical structure of the scale disappears, and the scale consists wholly of distincts. But this cannot be the case if there is in such scales a fusion of distinction with opposition; and looking closer we shall see that it is not the case.

26. The lowest member of the scale, the minimum realization of the generic essence, is already, so far as it goes, a realization of this essence, and therefore distinct from other realizations; but, as the limiting case, it is an extreme, and therefore an opposite relatively to the rest of the scale. Thus, if we try to form an idea of pure unmitigated wickedness, we find that, if we mean by this the complete absence of goodness—a zero in the scale of good—not only are there no extant examples of it, but we cannot even form a conception of it. The phrase, however useful as an expression of abhorrence, does not stand for any fact or even for any thought. A real case, or real conception, of extreme wickedness is a case or conception of some action or character which, however bad, is never wholly devoid of goodness, but possesses a goodness extremely low in degree and extremely low in kind. Here we stand in the scale of goodness not at zero, but at unity.

27. This minimum case of goodness is certainly, as one case of goodness, related to other cases by distinction; but, as a case extremely low in degree and kind, it is also related to them by opposition, as a case of the negation or privation of good and the presence of something hostile to good. It is not a thing whose moral nature, so far as it has any, is all goodness, in the same way in which the temperature of a very cold body is, so far as it goes, all heat. The character or act which possesses an extremely low

degree and kind of goodness is no less actual than one possessing a higher degree and kind; it does something, or is something, no less definite, and this something has a moral quality not completely described by calling it a very poor kind of good; we must go further and call it positively bad: the opposite of good.

Yet it has not two distinct attributes, goodness and badness, little of the one and much of the other. Its badness is nothing but its low degree and kind of goodness, conceived as opposed to higher degrees and kinds. Considered merely in itself, even this minimum case of goodness is good. There is no crime or vice which does not appear to the person who embraces it as good—good within its own limits and in the special way in which at the moment goodness appeals to him; no error so double-dyed that the person who falls into it does not for the time being think it true; no work of art so exquisitely false in taste that it may not be thought beautiful. The people who accept and admire these things are deceived, but not purely and simply deceived; we can see for ourselves, if we put ourselves at their point of view, that a person satisfied with so low a degree and kind of goodness, truth, or beauty is in these cases really getting what he asks, and is deceived only in thinking that goodness, truth, or beauty contains no more than that. The vice really does achieve something good: relief from pain, good fellowship, or a sense of emancipation. The error really does enshrine some truth, the bad work of art does contain some beauty.

All this is true when the minimum case is considered in itself. But when it is considered in relation to higher cases, all is changed. Pleasure in itself, so far as it goes, is good; but if the pursuit of pleasure is compared with the pursuit of duty, it becomes by comparison not merely less good, but positively evil. The lowest case in the scale, when compared with the next above it, not only loses its own intrinsic goodness and acquires the character of badness, but it actually becomes identical with evil in general; in it the abstract idea of evil finds a concrete embodiment, and at this point in the scale the achievement of goodness simply means the negation of this one thing. Examples are common and familiar. Every particular way of being good involves a struggle against some specific form of evil, some besetting sin; and in such a situation this besetting sin appears not as one alternative form of wrongdoing but as wrongdoing itself. Every achievement of truth involves combating some particular error, which again is regarded not as one among possible errors, still less as (what incidentally it always is) a partial and fragmentary truth, but as identical with error at large.

28. The same relation which subsists between the lowest member of the scale and the next above it reappears between any two adjacent forms. Each is good in itself, but bad in relation to the one above; and hence, wherever we stand on the scale, we are at a minimum point in it; and conversely, however far down we go, there is always the possibility of going lower without reaching absolute zero.

For a like reason we can always be sure that, when we have distinguished one single term or phase in the scale, closer scrutiny could break it up into a complex of sub-phases organized in the same general way. As applied to a philosophical subject-matter, simplicity and complexity are not mutually exclusive, they overlap; simplicity is only a relative term, and the complex, however deeply it is analysed, can only be analysed into parts that are still complex. Indeed, to think otherwise would imply that the terms of a philosophical series can be treated like a series of integers, and that would be to fall into the fallacy of calculation.

29. This view of the relation between the terms of a philosophical series, as a relation at once of distinction and of opposition, destroys two groups of errors: one asserting that because evil, error, and the like have actual existence in the world of experience, they are not negative but positive, standing to good, truth, &c., in a relation not of opposition but of mere distinction; the other asserting that because they are the negation of these positive terms they have no actuality, and that nothing evil exists. On the whole, the tradition of European philosophy (I have no right to speak of others) has kept clear of both fallacies, and has insisted that evil and error in themselves, as concepts, are privations, but that evils and errors are actual, and must be vigorously fought against. To waive the first contention for the sake of maintaining the second is to betray one of the fallacies I am here describing; to abandon the second

for its fancied inconsistency with the first is to betray the other.

The first may be called the fallacy of the false positive, because it consists in making a positive term out of what is really a negative one; the second the fallacy of null opposition, because it consists in placing the opposite of any positive term at the zero end of the scale. The dilemma of which these are the two horns is based on the false disjunction that if two terms are opposites they cannot be distincts (null opposition), and if distincts they cannot be opposites (false positive): the false disjunction of opposition and distinction.

§ 6

30. In the light of this further reinterpretation, we can return to the second defect revealed by the provisional scale of forms: namely, its failure to account for the overlap of classes.

The lower of any two adjacent terms is good in itself but bad relatively to its neighbour. Good and bad are here used merely illustratively; we might equally well use true and false, or any other such pair of terms. Now, the lower is not only good in general; it is good in a specific way; and if by comparison with its neighbour it loses its goodness, what it loses cannot be merely goodness in general; it must be this specific kind of goodness. What the higher term gains by the comparison, therefore, is again not merely goodness in general, but the specific kind of goodness proper to the lower. The higher term thus possesses not only that kind of goodness which belongs to it in its own right, but also the kind which originally or in itself belonged to its neighbour. It not only surpasses its neighbour in degree of goodness, but beats it, so to speak, on its own ground. The lower promises more than it can perform; it professes to exhibit a certain kind of goodness, but cannot in reality do so in a more than approximate and inadequate manner; just as it cannot wholly achieve goodness, so it cannot wholly achieve even that specific and admittedly imperfect form of it which is characteristically its own; this is genuinely achieved only by the next higher term, which professes to exhibit not this but the form next above it. Thus each term, which in itself is simply one specific form of goodness, has also a double relation to its neighbours: in comparison with the one below, it is what that professes to be; in comparison with the one above, it professes to be what that is.

This relation may be described, as here, by the metaphor of promising and performing; or it may be described by saying that the higher is the reality of which the lower is the appearance, or the ideal to which the lower is an approximation, or the truth of which the lower is a perversion. These are not so much metaphors as descriptions of something simpler and therefore more truly intelligible in terms of something more complex and, to us, more familiar. Promise and performance, appearance and reality, and the rest, all presuppose the relation which I am trying to describe; it is a purely logical relation, and unless we already understood it we could not understand the various relations in terms of which we try to explain it. As a purely logical relation, it is a synthesis of the four relations which it has been the task of this chapter to discuss: difference of degree, difference of kind, relation of distinction, and relation of opposition. The higher term is a species of the same genus as the lower, but it differs in degree as a more adequate embodiment of the generic essence, as well as in kind as a specifically different embodiment; it follows from this that it must be not only distinct from it, as one specification from another, but opposed to it, as a higher specification to a lower, a relatively adequate to a relatively inadequate, a true embodiment of the generic essence to a false embodiment; as true, it possesses not only its own specific character, but also that which its rival falsely claimed. The higher thus negates the lower, and at the same time reaffirms it: negates it as a false embodiment of the generic essence, and reaffirms its content, that specific form of the essence, as part and parcel of itself.

This conception of the higher term as beating the lower on its own ground has been here affirmed merely as a logical consequence of the principles already laid down; but it can be verified as a familiar fact wherever a philosophical scale of forms is recognized. If justice and expediency are adjacent terms in a scale of moral values, as we sometimes think them to be, it would follow that in order to secure expediency we must pass beyond mere expediency and rise to the level of justice; and this is a thought so familiar to us all that it is current as a proverb, honesty is the best policy. If, as St. Paul believed, law is given for the better ordering of life, and grace is something of the same general kind but a higher term in the same scale, it is no paradox that grace should perform exactly what law promised to perform but did not. If inference stands higher than judgement in a scale of the forms of thought, it is natural that inference should first give us what mere judgement cannot give, but ought to give if it is to be really judgement: knowledge, as opposed to mere opinion.

31. Each term in the scale, therefore, sums up the whole scale to that point. Wherever we stand in the scale, we stand at a culmination. Infinity as well as zero can thus be struck out of the scale, not because we never reach a real embodiment of the generic concept, but because the specific form at which we stand is the generic concept itself, so far as our thought yet conceives it. The proximate form, next below where we stand, is from this point of view at once the alternative possible way of specifying this concept, and the wrong way of specifying it; opposite to the way which we think the right way, and therefore opposite to the concept itself. What it endeavours to present as the whole of the concept is in reality an element within that whole, which, as an element in the culminating form, is reaffirmed in that form. All lower stages in the scale are

telescoped into this situation. They are in fact summed up in it twice over: once falsely, in the proximate specification, which misinterprets their significance and combines them into a false unity, and once truly, in the culminating form.

32. This explains the overlap of classes in a philosophical genus. The higher of any two adjacent forms overlaps the lower because it includes the positive content of the lower as a constituent element within itself. It only fails to include the lower in its entirety because there is also a negative aspect of the lower, which is rejected by the higher: the lower, in addition to asserting its own content, denies that the generic essence contains anything more, and this denial constitutes its falsehood. Thus, utilitarianism is right to regard expediency as one form of goodness; its mistake is to think that there is nothing in even the highest forms of goodness that cannot be described in terms of expediency; and therefore a better moral philosophy would reaffirm utilitarianism while denying one part, this negative part, of its doctrine.

The lower overlaps the higher in a different sense: it does not include the higher as part of itself, it adopts part of the positive content of the higher, while rejecting another part. Utilitarianism, for example, claims much of the contents of better moral theories as sound utilitarian doctrine, but dismisses the rest as so much error or superstition. What is true of utilitarianism as a specific kind of moral theory is true also of expediency as a specific kind of goodness. Duty rejects expediency in the sense of refusing to accept it as even a legitimate kind of goodness, and regarding it rather as the inveterate enemy of morality, but reaffirms it in the sense of accepting it, when modified by subordination to its own principles, as a constituent element in itself. Thus duty and expediency overlap: a dutiful action always has its own expediency, and an expedient action to that extent partakes of the nature of duty.

33. These considerations not only show how an overlap of classes is possible, but make it clearer than before what exactly this overlap is. It is not merely that some dutiful actions are expedient, leaving a margin of expedient actions that are not dutiful and dutiful actions that are not expedient. All dutiful actions are expedient, for duty as the higher specification always and necessarily reaffirms the lower; and the lower not sometimes but always partially and incompletely affirms the higher. The overlap consists in this, that the lower is contained in the higher, the higher transcending the lower and adding to it something new, whereas the lower partially coincides with the higher, but differs from it in rejecting this increment. Thus the overlap is essentially not, as we took it to be in our first rough survey of the ground, an overlap of extension between classes, but an overlap of intension between concepts, each in its degree a specification of their generic essence, but each embodying it more adequately than the one below.

IV

DEFINITION AND DESCRIPTION

1. In the two foregoing chapters I have tried to show that the doctrines of classification and division, as contained in traditional logic, are neither simply true nor simply false when applied to the concepts of philosophy; but that they have been framed rather with an eye to the peculiar structure of the scientific concept, and must be modified in certain ways before they can be applied to the philosophical. In this chapter I shall argue that the same is true of definition. I am here discussing what is called real, as opposed to verbal, definition: not the definition of words but the definition of concepts.

It has generally been held in the past that philosophical concepts can and ought to be defined. It was in fact by insisting upon definition that Socrates is believed to have won his unique place in the history of philosophical method. But there is a curious paradox in our accounts of what Socrates taught. He believed that all philosophical concepts ought to be defined, but this belief expressed not an achievement but an ideal in the light of which he was forced to admit that he knew nothing except his own ignorance. For, challenging himself to produce adequate definitions of philosophical concepts, he found himself unable to do so.

2. The examples which we possess of Socrates' search for definitions make it clear that, when he

asked himself or his pupils to define a concept, the model which he held up for imitation was definition as it exists in mathematics. This no doubt accounts for his failure; and it also accounts for the tendency which exists at the present time to deny that philosophical concepts admit of definition. It is pointed out that when we attempt to define a philosophical concept either we introduce into the definition the term to be defined, and so commit the formal fallacy of *circulus in definiendo*, or else, avoiding that danger, we fare worse and fall into the material falsehood of substituting in the definition another concept for that which we set out to define.

All this is true and unanswerable if definition is taken to mean what it means in mathematics; and if the word definition is by custom of language confined to that meaning, the philosophical concept must be called indefinable. But this is a dangerous doctrine. It leaves philosophy defenceless against any one who chooses to claim a perfect and infallible knowledge which, since it cannot be expressed in words, he need not be at the trouble of stating. The incentive given by such doctrine to careless thinking and obscure expression, and the handicap it lays upon candid and critical philosophizing, make it a serious danger to thought. A doctrine need not be false because it is dangerous; but its danger is a warning that its credentials should be examined with scrupulous care before it is accepted.

They will not bear examination. The word to define and its cognates are legitimately but not exclusively used in this special sense. To define is literally to fix the limits of a plot of land or the like, to show where one thing begins and another ends, or in general to discriminate or distinguish. A person asked to define his position, in an argument, is being asked to remove ambiguities from a statement of it which, implicitly or explicitly, he is understood to have made, and thus make it clearer and more precise. A photographic image is said to be ill-defined when the degree of blurring is more than can reasonably be permitted. In these ordinary or common-sense uses of the word, it is implied that definition is a matter of degree: to define is not to make absolutely definite what was absolutely indefinite, but to make more definite what was to some extent definite already.

3. As applied in exact science, definition carries a special meaning. Definitions here define absolutely. A person possessing a definition knows the essence of the concept perfectly, one who does not possess it does not know that essence at all. In order that this should be possible, two conditions must be fulfilled. First, the essence must be something capable of final and exhaustive statement, and therefore sharply cut off from mere properties. Secondly, an equally sharp line must be drawn between knowing something and not knowing it. Owing to the differences in the structure of their concepts, both these conditions are fulfilled in exact science, neither in philosophy.

A definition in exact science states the essence as

distinct from the properties; these, which flow logically from the essence, are stated in theorems. The exposition of the concept as a whole thus consists of definition and theorems taken together. The reason why it can be divided into these two parts is that, owing to the logical structure of the concept, one part can be expounded without any fear that it may have to be reconsidered when we come to expound the rest.

4. Suppose there were a kind of concept which could not be so divided as to be expounded in this way: a kind of concept in expounding which the later part of the exposition, instead of depending upon the earlier as upon a fixed point, served to qualify or explain the earlier. In the case of such a concept no line could be drawn between definition and theorems; the entire exposition would be a statement at once of its essence, and of its properties regarded as the elements constituting that essence. This would be a definition, for it would state the essence; the concept would remain undefined only in the sense that there would be no one phrase or sentence which could be taken out of its context and called the definition.

This is the case in philosophy. It must be so, if the species of a philosophical genus overlap; for essence and property are two species of attribute, and definitions and theorems are two corresponding species of exposition; in a philosophical context, therefore, these species will overlap. And experience of philosophical thought shows that it is so. An essay on a philosophical concept like justice does not ordinarily begin with a definition of the concept and go on by deducing theorems about it; it consists from beginning to end of an attempt to expound the concept in a statement which may properly be described as an extended and reasoned definition.

5. The second condition of definition, in the special sense in which exact science uses the word, is that there should be an absolute difference between knowing a concept and not knowing it. In exact science there appears to be this difference. At the beginning of a lesson, it may never have occurred to the pupil that there can be a twelve-sided regular solid. In the course of the lesson he may come to know that there is such a thing, and that its name is dodecahedron. His knowledge of its essence is now complete, however much he has still to learn about its properties.

6. Suppose there were a kind of knowledge in which a distinction existed between knowing better and knowing worse, but none between knowing absolutely and not knowing at all. In pursuing this knowledge, we should begin not with utter ignorance of the subject-matter or any part of it, but with a dim and confused knowledge, or a knowledge definite enough in some parts but confused in others, and in others fading away to the verge of complete nescience. In advancing our knowledge of these things we should say, not 'I have discovered something that I never knew before', but 'I have cleared up my thoughts about this matter, and see that what

I once thought about it was a confused mixture of truth and error.' In this kind of knowledge there would be no need for definitions like that of the dodecahedron, for there would be no occasion on which we were absolutely ignorant of any concept contained in its subject-matter; nor any possibility of them, for we could never come to a point at which our knowledge concerning the essence of a concept could be described as complete.

This also is the case in philosophy. It must be so, if the philosophical concept is specified in a scale of forms; for knowledge itself, as understood in philosophy, will form such a scale, in which all ignorance is a lower or more rudimentary kind of knowledge, and the zero of absolute ignorance is never reached. And any one with any experience of philosophy knows that in fact it is so. The beginner in philosophy finds himself listening to discussions about right and wrong, truth and error, pleasure and pain, and the like. If he said to his teacher, 'I do not know what right and wrong are; please give me a definition of them before proceeding with the discussion,' the teacher would reply, 'I am trying to give you a definition of them as fast as I can; and if you did not learn in the nursery enough about the nature of right and wrong to follow my discussion, you had better go back to the nursery again.' For in all philosophical study we begin by knowing something about the subject-matter, and on that basis go on to learn more; at each step we re-define our concept by way of recording our progress; and the process can end only when the definition states all that the concept contains.

7. Definition as thus understood resembles the definition of exact science in stating the concept's essence; and that, after all, is the essence of definition. But there are some traditional rules of definition which it will honour more in the breach than the observance: namely those (there are several in the text-books) which apply only to the special case of exact science. Thus, if judgement is defined as the reference of an ideal content to reality, this may be criticized on the ground of circularity, because to refer means to judge; but that is a fault only if the definition is addressed to a person who has never thought about the nature of judgement. To a person who has already thought about a given concept, definitions of it which formal logic would condemn as circular, metaphorical, or obscure may be of the utmost value.

8. In stating an essence which is identified not with one selected part of the concept but with the concept as a whole, philosophical definition resembles the descriptions which take the place of definitions in empirical science. A person asked to describe an elephant or a comet—not an individual elephant or an individual comet, but the concept—would aim at completeness: he would try to include in his exposition all the attributes properly included in the concept. This exposition of an empirical concept cannot be accurately divided into exposition of essence (definition) and exposition of properties

(theorems), because the logical connexions upon which that division rests are lacking. There is no one attribute of a comet or an elephant from which we can deduce all the rest; we do not sufficiently understand the way in which their various attributes are interconnected; and so, from our point of view, these attributes tend to form a mere aggregate in which certain elements are found together without any reason why they should be together. This tendency is no doubt opposed by another, tending to connect the attributes into a logical whole; so that the description of an empirical concept is in general an ambiguous thing: partly it approximates to the exposition of a mathematical concept in which some one attribute is essential and the others flow from it; partly it approximates to a mere enumeration of attributes which in actual experience are found together, we cannot tell why.

The exposition of a philosophical concept has a certain resemblance to this. Both alike aim at completeness and renounce the attempt to select one element and call it essence, leaving the rest to be deduced from it. But they renounce this for opposite reasons. An empirical description does so because we do not well enough understand the logical structure of the concept; a philosophical exposition, because we understand it too well to rest content with a separation which must to a great extent be arbitrary. We may, if we like to insist on this resemblance, say that a philosophical exposition describes its subject-matter; but that would be misleading unless it were made clear that describing in this case means not merely enumerating the items of which the subject-matter is composed but expounding them in such a way as to exhibit their connexions.

To follow such an exposition means gradually building up in one's mind the conception which is being expounded; coming to know it better and better as each new point is made, and at each new point summing up the whole exposition to that point. The thought of the subject-matter is thus gradually becoming clearer and more complete. But this is not a mere change in degree. It must be a change in kind also. The fresh points are not merely closer and closer approximations to the truth, like fresh decimal places; they are qualitatively new as well; and hence the phases through which the definition passes in its growth are not only new in degree, as we come to know the concept better, but new in kind, as we come to grasp fresh aspects of it. The various phases will therefore constitute a scale of forms, beginning with a rudimentary or minimum definition and adding qualitatively new determinations which gradually alter the original definition so as to make it a better and better statement of the concept's essence: a statement, at each step, complete as far as it goes, and expressing a real and necessary specification of the concept.

9. To define a philosophical concept, therefore, it is necessary first to think of that concept as speci-

fying itself in a form so rudimentary that anything less would fail to embody the concept at all. This will be the minimum specification of the concept, the lower end of the scale; and the first phase of the definition will consist in stating this. Later phases will modify this minimum definition by adding new determinations, each implied in what went before, but each introducing into it qualitative changes as well as additions and complications. Finally, a phase will be reached in which the definition contains, explicitly stated, all that can be found in the concept; the definition is now adequate to the thing defined and the process is as complete as we can make it.

This definition of a philosophical concept by means of a scale of forms is a method repeatedly used throughout the history of philosophy; it will suffice to quote a few of the most familiar examples. Plato in the *Republic* sets himself the task of defining the 'city' (there is no word in ordinary English that adequately translates πόλις). He begins by offering a definition of the 'minimum city' (ἀναγκαιοτάτη πόλις), which is reduced to a minimum in two ways: first all functions other than economic are ignored, and then the economic functions are reduced to the barest development necessary to sustain life. He then proceeds to develop the concept, first by adding luxuries to necessaries, and then by adding to the economic function the military and political; and the concept becomes complete when all these have been considered singly and the relations between them worked out in detail. It is instructive to remember that Aristotle modified Plato's definition chiefly by taking the minimum one stage lower. Plato assumed that a family is not a city at all, and that the minimum city consists of a number of producers each with a family of his own; Aristotle finds the germ of political life within the family itself, and traces a progressive evolution of the concept of 'society' (*κοινωνία*) from that germ to its fullest realization in the complete city state.

Aristotle understood the method well; he not only uses it himself, for example in his methodical exposition of the nature of life,[1] he criticizes Plato for not having used it enough; for, says he, Plato's Socrates laughed at Gorgias for offering a whole series of specific forms of 'virtue' when asked for a unitary definition of 'virtue'; but the Socratic attempt at a unitary definition was even more faulty, neglecting as it did the specific forms of the concept. Accordingly, Aristotle spaces out the generic concept of 'virtue' on a scale in which the first specific form considered is the lowest, that of the slave (the context is political), and so an ascent is made—roughly and unsystematically, it is true—to the higher forms.[2]

10. One example from modern philosophy will suffice. In the *Grundlegung zur Metaphysik der Sitten*, Kant sets himself to answer the question what the word good means when applied in the specifically moral sense to a good man or a good act. His answer falls into three main stages. First, he argues that a

[1] *De Anima*. [2] *Politics*, 1259 B, 20 seqq.

good act is one in which we obey a rule conceived as universally binding. This is the minimum definition of a good act, not the whole definition; it is soon modified so as to appear in a second and more elaborate form: a good act is one in which we treat human nature as an end in itself. This is more elaborate because it is in effect the same definition modified by adding to the notion of objective rationality (a universal rule) the notion of subjective rationality (human nature as rational and therefore demanding the same kind of respect which we give to rationality as such). The third definition introduces a further complication, namely the idea of other rational beings treating us in the same way in which we treat them; thus the second definition, reciprocally applied, becomes the third: a good act is one in which we act as members of a kingdom of ends, or society in which every one is both subject (as respecting the wills of others) and sovereign (as counting upon the same respect in them). Hegel, who used this method throughout his philosophical works, might be suspected of having borrowed it from the Greeks, but the same suspicion cannot fall on Kant, who was very little influenced by Greek thought. He rediscovered it for himself by developing the methods he had learnt from the Cartesians; and it is in fact to him, rather than to the Greeks, that his successors owed it.

V

THE PHILOSOPHICAL JUDGEMENT: QUALITY AND QUANTITY

1. THE foregoing chapters have dealt, not exhaustively but perhaps sufficiently for the reader's patience, with some of the chief points in which the universals or concepts of philosophy differ from those of exact and empirical science. According to the doctrine of traditional logic, which on this matter need not here be disputed, the concept is a logical element only found within something more complex, called a judgement or proposition; and this, therefore, is the subject that next demands our notice. The procedure will be as before: to ask how the judgements or propositions of philosophy (the two words may be taken, for the present purpose, as synonymous) differ from those of science in respect of logical structure.

The traditional theory of judgement falls into four sections under the heads of quality, quantity, relation, and modality. This chapter will be devoted to quality and quantity; that is, it will discuss the way in which the terms affirmative and negative, universal and particular, apply to the judgements of philosophy. In the following chapter, relation will be considered. Concerning modality I have nothing to say except what is said by implication in the chapters next after that.

§ I

2. According to quality, judgements are divided into affirmative and negative. It has already been

remarked in an earlier chapter that these classes always to some extent overlap: many judgements, perhaps all, contain both an affirmative and a negative element. But in the case of philosophical statements the relation between affirmation and negation is peculiarly intimate. On a matter of empirical fact it is possible, when asked for example 'where did I leave my purse?' to answer 'not in the taxi, I am sure', without having the least idea where the purse was actually left. That negative judgement contains affirmative implications; for example, 'if you had left your purse in the taxi I should have noticed it'; but these do not include an affirmative answer to the question which has been answered in the negative.

In philosophy this is not so. The normal and natural way of replying to a philosophical statement from which we dissent is by saying, not simply 'this view seems to me wrong', but 'the truth, I would suggest, is something more like this', and then we should attempt to state a view of our own. This view certainly need not be on the tip of our tongue; it may be something with which our mind, as Socrates would say, is pregnant, and which needs both skill and pains to bring it to birth; yet we feel it quick within us; and unless we have that feeling we have no right to meddle with the question that is being discussed; no right, and if we have the spirit of a philosopher no desire.

3. This is not a mere opinion. It is a corollary of the Socratic principle (itself a necessary consequence of the principle of overlapping classes) that there is

in philosophy no such thing as a transition from sheer ignorance to sheer knowledge, but only a progress in which we come to know better what in some sense we know already. It follows from this that when we discover a new truth we recognize it as something which we have always known; and that when we are still in pursuit of such a truth we know already, if we understand the nature of philosophical thought, that we are only relatively and not absolutely ignorant of it.

4. Consequently we can never in philosophy decline, except temporarily and provisionally, the duty of giving our own affirmative answer to any question which others have answered in ways that we regard as false. To reject one account of a philosophical matter is to accept the responsibility of giving a better account of it; and hence in philosophy, whatever may be the case elsewhere, it is a rule of sound method that every negation in this special sense implies an affirmation. This rule may be called the principle of concrete negation, and the neglect of it the fallacy of abstract negation.

5. There is also a principle of concrete affirmation and a corresponding fallacy of abstract affirmation.

Every affirmative judgement no doubt contains some negative elements; but in a philosophical judgement there is a peculiar intimacy in the relation between the two kinds of element. The negative elements give point to our affirmations by indicating what exactly they are intended to deny. For every philosophical statement is intended to express the rejection of some definite proposition which the person making the statement regards as erroneous. In non-philosophical thought this is not necessarily the case. When I say 'the molecule of water contains two atoms of hydrogen and one of oxygen' or 'the battle of Hastings was fought in 1066', I am doubtless denying something; but there is no one particular error, such as that the formula of water is HO_2 or that the battle of Hastings was fought in 1087, against which I am putting myself or my hearer on guard. But when I make a philosophical statement, such as that the species of a philosophical genus overlap, I am denying something perfectly definite: the proposition that they are mutually exclusive. Thus a non-philosophical judgement, when it affirms, denies indiscriminately all the judgements incompatible with it; a philosophical judgement, when it affirms, picks out some one incompatible judgement, focuses itself on the denial of that, and by this denial comes to focus or define its own precise significance.

6. The reason for this lies in the logical structure of the concept. Any judgement predicates a concept, and whenever we affirm one specific concept we deny the other specifications of the same genus. 'The book which I am looking for is green'; here, what is denied is that the book is blue, brown, or any other specific colour. Where the generic concept is non-philosophical, as here, the affirmation of one specific form involves the indiscriminate denial of all the rest, for their structure is that of a group of co-ordinate classes where each excludes each and

therefore any one excludes all the rest, none more than another. But where the generic concept is philosophical, specified in a scale of forms of which the judgement is intended to affirm the highest (which it always is, because every one necessarily conceives the highest specific form known to him as the true form of the generic concept, and so affirms that), its denial of all the inferior forms is summarized in one denial, namely that of the proximate form; since each summarizes the whole scale up to that point, and the denial of that involves the denial of all that it summarizes. What is true in the proximate form, and therefore in all the lower forms, is still contained in the highest form; hence the proximate form as contrasted with the highest is nothing but a compendium of all the errors which in asserting the highest form we mean to deny.

Hence the statement that a philosophical assertion whenever it affirms something definite also denies something definite, records not a mere fact observed in our experience of philosophy, but a principle of method. Empirically, cases can perhaps be found in which a philosopher makes an assertion with no very clear idea of what he means to deny. But if so, he is committing the fallacy of abstract affirmation; and though it is doubtless possible to think what is substantially true while yet thinking in terms of this fallacy, the truth is attained not because of, but in spite of, the principles employed in the search.

7. The principle of concrete affirmation, as the denial of this fallacy, can be applied in two ways.

As applied to one's own thought, it runs: 'If you want to be clear as to what you are asserting, be clear as to what you are denying.' In other words, it is never enough to state your aim in a special philosophical inquiry by saying that you wish to discover the truth about a particular subject; this must always be further defined by adding that you wish to discover what exactly is wrong with this or that view of it. And this implies that without systematic and painstaking analysis of false views, to discover where they are false, there is in philosophy no reaching any truth that is worth reaching.

The principle also applies to our comprehension of others' thoughts. Here it runs thus: 'In reading or listening to a philosopher, never be content to ask yourself what he means to affirm, without at the same time asking what he means to deny.' It is of great importance to observe this rule in our philosophical reading; important because difficult; for the great philosophers of the past, whose works stand like islands out of continents otherwise submerged by the waters of time, have formed their own views by criticizing others that have not come down to us except so far as we can reconstruct them from these same criticisms. Yet, if we cannot understand what the doctrines were which a Plato or a Parmenides meant to deny, it is certain that to just that extent we are unable to grasp what it was that he meant to affirm.

It does not follow that every philosophical assertion is directed against some view which some one actually holds. A view need not have been affirmed, in order to be worth denying; all that is necessary is that it should be plausible, a view for which there are reasons, though not sufficient reasons. This implies that the rejected view must seem plausible to the person who rejects it; so that, if its rejection implies controversy, it is a controversy not so much between two philosophers as within the mind of a single one: a dialogue, as Plato called it, of the soul with itself. In confirmation of this, one often finds philosophical writers of intelligence qualifying their controversial passages by saying: The view to which I object is, on the face of it, the view of such and such a person; but if I am mistaken in thinking he holds it, let me be understood as dissenting not from a philosopher, but from a philosophy.'

8. Taking these two principles together, it may be said that whereas outside philosophy a judgement is either affirmative or negative, though not exclusively either, since each may have in it elements of the other, in philosophy there is such a balance of the two that no properly weighed and considered judgement is more affirmative than negative or more negative than affirmative. The affirmative judgement in philosophy runs thus: S is P and not Q; the negative thus: S is not Q but P; where P and Q are equally definite and specific answers to the same question: what is S? The peculiarity of the philosophical judgement in respect of quality, then, lies in the peculiar intimacy of the relation between its affirmative and negative elements, which is of such

a kind that P cannot be validly affirmed while Q is left indeterminate, nor Q validly denied while P is left indeterminate.

§ 2

9. In respect of quantity, judgements are traditionally divided into universal, particular, and singular. The judgements of philosophy, like those of science, are universal; but we have to ask whether there may not be some special shade of meaning expressed by the term universal in this context.

The species universal, particular, and singular naturally overlap; the universal judgement that all men are mortal does not exclude, it includes, the particular judgement that some men are mortal and the singular judgement that this individual man Socrates is mortal. These three elements introduce differentiations into its significance, even considered as a universal judgement: as a pure universal, it means that man as such is mortal; as a universal of particulars, it means that every kind of man is mortal; as a universal of singulars it means that every individual man is mortal. These are not so much three kinds of universal judgement as three elements present in every universal judgement whether in philosophy or anywhere else.

10. But these three elements are differently related in different types of universal judgement. There is one kind of thought in which the determining element is the singular. Each individual instance of S is found on examination to be P; and, since we cannot think this a mere coincidence, we regard

ourselves as justified in thinking that they are P only because they are S; that is to say, S as such is P. Here the singular element is primary, the universal secondary. A universal judgement of this kind is called a generalization. It is a common and indeed indispensable type of judgement, although logicians have frowned upon it as *inductio per enumerationem simplicem.*

A second type begins not from the singular but from the particular: primarily it judges that each particular kind of S is P, and thence it goes on to judge that S as such is P. This is the type of universal judgement which is normal in empirical science, where the importance of the plurality of instances towards establishing a universal proposition lies not in their numerical difference, as in generalization proper, but in the specific differences between them.

A third type takes the universal element as primary: we begin by thinking that S as such is P, and this is seen to involve the particular, that any specific kind of S is P, and the singular, that each instance of S is P. This is the type of universal judgement which obtains in exact science. When we assert a property of a triangle, we assert it ordinarily in the illustrative case of an individual triangle which is also a triangle of a particular kind; but our assertion in no way rests either on its individual or on its particular features, but only on those which belong to it as a triangle; that is, the assertion is primarily made about triangles as such.

11. In philosophical judgements, universal as they are, the same three elements are necessarily present; but none of these three types of structure will serve. Let us look at them in turn.

Suppose a philosopher is in the act of making up his mind to a universal judgement, for example that acts are right in so far as they promote happiness. If this judgement were in the nature of a generalization, the procedure in forming it would be first to observe that many individual right acts promote happiness, and then to presume that their being right is either identical, or in some way specially connected, with their 'felicific' property. But no competent philosopher argues in this way, and with good reason; for since the concept in question is a philosophical one, the acts which he describes (no doubt correctly) as right may also be, for example, expedient or benevolent; and it may be this, rather than their rightness, that is connected with their promoting happiness. In short, to frame a universal judgement in philosophy by generalization from instances is to commit the fallacy of identified coincidents; and if the instances are so selected as to avoid that, the result will be the fallacy of precarious margins.

Suppose, then, he proceeds as in empirical science: treats the concept as a genus, distinguishes its various species, and looks for the generic essence in the shape of something common to these species and indifferently present in them all. Thus, trying to determine the general nature of knowledge, he might assume that anything which could be called knowledge at all, however humble or elementary a kind of knowledge, could be relied upon to exhibit that general nature as well as any other. Philosophers as it were instinctively avoid this way of approaching a question, because they feel that the full nature of anything is exemplified only in the highest forms of it; what is to be found in the lowest forms is not the generic essence in its completeness, but only the minimum form of it; and because the lower in a scale of forms is in some sense opposed to the higher, they realize that a theory proceeding on this assumption is likely to find itself maintaining that the highest forms of knowledge, morality, art, and so forth are not forms of knowledge and the like at all.

Thirdly, suppose he begins by convincing himself that the concept with which he is dealing has certain attributes, and goes on by forcing these attributes upon every specification and every instance of it; for example, suppose he begins by deciding that action as such is the pursuit of the agent's own pleasure, and in the light of this universal proposition insists that a martyr going to the stake must be at bottom pursuing his own pleasure, though admittedly that is not the most natural account of his action. The reason why this procedure is bad philosophy is that although a certain hedonistic element does run like a thread through every form of action, it plays different parts in different forms: in some it is a predominant motive, in others it is present only as something to be fought against. Any statement about a generic concept which is true as applied to one of its specific forms is likely to require modification before it can be applied to any other; without such modification it is likely to be not so much false as misleading, perverse, or wantonly paradoxical.

12. In order to avoid these three fallacies it is necessary, not to look for a fourth way of arranging the three elements of the universal judgement, but to use all three methods at once, checking each by means of the others. All three types of structure are to be found in the philosophical judgement; what is not found is any sufficiency of one to the exclusion of the rest. In framing a philosophical judgement, therefore, we take up each aspect in turn, and reserve judgement on each until we are satisfied with all.

Philosophy can and does generalize, or assert of the concept as such what is found in its single instances; but subject to the provision that, by itself, this is only a clue towards answering its question, not a substantive answer. Thus, examples seem to show that certain constant features appear in all works of art; but this by itself does not answer the question whether they are features necessarily belonging to art as such.

Again, like empirical science, philosophy can and does argue that if different species of a concept agree in a certain respect this should be a feature belonging to the generic essence; but this again gives only clues, not substantive definitions; they must be checked by arranging the species in a scale and showing that the features of the generic essence shine out more clearly as the scale reaches its culmination.

Lastly, philosophy like exact science aims at determining *a priori* the characteristics which belong of necessity to its concepts as such in their true universality. But in philosophy every statement of this kind is merely tentative until it has been verified by reference to the facts: a philosophical theory must show that what it claims as necessary in the concept is possible in every specification of the concept and actual in its instances.

But we are already touching the frontier that separates the theory of judgement from the theory of inference; and the problems of method that have been briefly indicated in these paragraphs must await a fuller discussion until we come to consider the relation of philosophical reasoning to that of deductive and inductive science.

VI
PHILOSOPHY AS CATEGORICAL THINKING

§ 1

1. In order to assert a proposition in mathematics, it is not necessary to believe that the subject of discourse has any actual existence. We say that every square has its diagonals equal; but to say this we need not think that we have any acquaintance with actual squares. It is no shock to our geometrical knowledge to realize that the perceptible objects passing by that name are only approximately square, and that if by any chance—which is infinitely unlikely—one of them did happen to be a true square, we could never tell it from the rest, and therefore could not base our geometrical knowledge on special study of it.

Nor need we hold that, though in the perceptible world no squares are to be found, they exist in an intelligible world. That is a metaphysical conception full of difficulties; a thing far harder to conceive than the notions of elementary geometry; a theory to which the Greeks were driven by reflection on their mathematical knowledge, but one which to the Greeks as a people, and to each of ourselves as individuals, came after a grounding in mathematics, not before it.

What is necessary is not to believe that a square anywhere or in any sense exists, but to suppose it. Given a rough chalk diagram, we must be able to suppose these broad and crooked marks to be straight lines, suppose these lines equal, and suppose each to be connected with its neighbours by a right angle. We can suppose what we know to be not the case; we can even suppose what we know to be impossible, whether accidentally, as we can suppose Napoleon to have won the battle of Waterloo, or inherently, as when we invite some one to 'suppose that a fairy gave you three wishes'. In mathematics we frame a supposition and then see what follows from it; this complex thought is called in logic a hypothetical proposition; and it is of such propositions that the body of mathematical knowledge is composed.

Here I distinguish the body of mathematical knowledge from certain other things, necessary perhaps to its existence, but not part and parcel of it. For example, it may or may not be necessary, in geometry, to perceive or imagine a figure; I do not ask whether it is or not; but if it is, this perceiving or imagining is only a *conditio sine qua non* of geometrical knowledge, not geometrical knowledge itself. It may or may not be necessary to understand certain logical principles according to which geometrical reasoning proceeds; if it is, the knowledge of these principles is not geometrical knowledge. If the reader distinguishes between mathematical knowledge itself and all these accessories or conditions or concomitants of it, he will, I think, be satisfied that mathematics itself consists exclusively of hypothetical propositions.

2. Empirical science notoriously deals not with

abstractions, but with facts; and therefore its universal statements might be thought wholly devoid of this hypothetical element. And certainly, when a pathologist or bacteriologist talks of tuberculosis, he is talking of facts that are actual, of a disease that exists and from which people really die. But the scientist is not concerned simply with bare facts in all their multiform variety. He is also and especially concerned with a certain framework into which he fits them, grouping them round fixed points and treating these fixed points as foci of his thought. The framework is no doubt altered from time to time, at the suggestion of the facts themselves; there is no question of forcing the facts into a frame constructed altogether *a priori*; but without such a framework there is no science. Tuberculosis is not a name for all the infinite varieties of clinical phenomena which the tubercle bacillus can produce, it is the name of a specific disease or 'entity', a certain set of standard symptoms with a standard history, to which all these varieties more or less conform. The entity of tuberculosis is thus one fixed point in a framework, or system of medicine, into which the individual cases encountered in medical practice must be fitted.

Now, just as a man, after plotting a number of observations on squared paper, may summarize their distribution by drawing a curve which represents their general tendency but need not pass through a single one of the points actually plotted, so the writer of a medical text-book may compose the description of a standard case of a certain disease, bearing in mind the varieties which cases referred to that disease exhibit in clinical experience, but not describing any case that he has ever actually seen. And this description may be of service in the training of other physicians, even if they too never meet a case corresponding precisely, point by point, with the text-book. But the business of the text-book is to describe this or that disease, as an entity; therefore the individual cases, in so far as they do not exactly correspond with the text-book description, are not exactly instances of the entity described: they are complicated cases, or abnormal cases, or in one way or another not true cases of the disease as described in the text-book. This is not because the text-book is a bad text-book; it is a necessary consequence from the very notion of a specific disease; nor is it a peculiarity of medical science; it belongs to the logical structure of empirical science in general. There is no difference in this respect between the conception of a specific disease and the conception of a specific plant.

It follows that the universal propositions laid down by empirical science have a hypothetical character not unlike that of mathematical propositions. The statement in a medical or botanical text-book that all cases of tuberculosis or all rosaceae have these and these characteristics, turns out to mean that the standard case has them; but it does not follow that the standard case exists; it may be a mere *ens rationis*; and since that would not disturb the truth of the original statement, it follows that the original statement was in intention hypothetical.

As in exact science, so here in empirical, the body of knowledge must be distinguished from certain necessary or fortuitous accompaniments of it. The accurate observation and record of facts is most necessary to empirical science; and the propositions in which these facts are expressed are categorical: for example, that the patient's temperature has been this or that at such and such a time. And the application of scientific knowledge to individual cases involves another kind of categorical proposition: for example, that the patient is suffering from tuberculosis. But the body of scientific knowledge is expressed in propositions that are logically intermediate between these two orders of categoricals, the statements of fact which are its data and the statements of fact which are its applications; and this body itself consists of hypothetical propositions.

3. Philosophical thought differs in this respect both from mathematics and from empirical science. The body or substance of it is composed of propositions which instead of being merely hypothetical are in essence and fundamental intention categorical.

I hope in the sequel to satisfy the reader not only that this has been the view taken by philosophers themselves, but also that it follows necessarily from the hypothesis which we have agreed to explore. But before doing this I must shortly consider certain reasons which might induce him, on encountering the opinion just expressed, to reject it out of hand as an obvious error.

First, we sometimes call a statement categorical, meaning only that it is made with conviction. In that sense, the proper place for categorical judgements is in connexion with subject-matters where it is either easy to arrive at the truth, or imperative to make up our minds even on evidence logically inadequate; but there is perhaps no subject in which truth is so hard to find as in philosophy, and it is a subject in which no practical urgency can excuse a hasty judgement; it is therefore the last place in the world where we can afford to be, in that sense, categorical. All our judgements in philosophy should be peculiarly cautious, tentative, slowly formed, and expressed with all possible reserve and qualification. But I am using the word categorical in the logician's sense, not the popular sense just defined. The question I am discussing is what logical form philosophical knowledge would take if we could achieve it, not the question how easy it is to achieve.

Secondly, a person who understands the essentially hypothetical nature of all scientific knowledge, and this is a conception with which most people in our time are familiar, naturally tends to think that the same is true of philosophy. It is a reasonable presumption that whatever is true of science is true of philosophy, and merely as a presumption it deserves all respect; but every one admits that there are differences between them, and the subject of this essay is the general question what these differences are. I must therefore ask the reader to approach this particular aspect of the question with an open mind.

§ 2

4. That the aim of philosophy is in the last resort to formulate its thought categorically, is a principle repeated by philosophers of all times in the most varied manners. Thus Plato, discussing the difference between dialectic and mathematics in a passage already quoted (*Rep.* 511 B), explains that whereas the starting-points of mathematical reasoning are mere hypotheses, dialectic demands for itself a 'non-hypothetical starting-point' (ἀρχὴ ἀνυποθέτος). The question how Plato thought that this demand could be satisfied is full of difficulties and obscurities; but the purport of the demand itself is clear.

Aristotle states the same principle in a way so different that we can hardly suppose him to be copying Plato. In the work which has given its name to the science of metaphysics, he defines his subject-matter as reality or being (*Met.* 993 A 30: ἡ περὶ τῆς ἀληθείας θεωρία, 1003 A 20: ἐπιστήμη τις ἣ θεωρεῖ τὸ ὄν ᾗ ὄν).

In modern times one might quote Kant's dictum that in a critique of pure reason 'anything in the nature of a hypothesis must be treated as contraband', or Hegel's declaration that the subject-matter of philosophy is no mere thought and no mere abstraction but *die Sache selbst*. But *obiter dicta* cannot decide philosophical questions; indeed, if they could, there would be some plausibility in the notion that what we are discussing in philosophy is not *die Sache selbst* but only thoughts, the thoughts that philosophers have had about it.

5. More to the point than a collection of opinions would be a consideration of one famous argument which has stood in the forefront of metaphysical discussion for nearly nine hundred years: the Ontological Proof.

Plato had long ago laid it down that to be, and to be knowable, are the same (*Rep.* 476 E); and, in greater detail, that a thought cannot be a mere thought, but must be a thought of something, and of something real (ὄντος, *Parm.* 132 B). The neo-Platonists had worked out the conception of God in the metaphysical sense of the word—a being of whom we can say *est id quod est*, a unity of existence and essence, a perfect being (*pulcherrimum fortissimumque*) such that *nihil deo melius excogitari queat* (the phrases are from Boethius, *De Trinitate*).

Anselm, putting these two thoughts together, the original Platonic principle that when we really think (but when do we really think, if ever?) we must be thinking of a real object, and the neo-Platonic idea of a perfect being (something which we cannot help conceiving in our minds; but does that guarantee it more than a mere idea?), or rather, pondering on the latter thought until he rediscovered the former as latent within it, realized that to think of this perfect being at all was already to think of him, or it, as existing.

Divesting his argument of all specially religious or theological colouring, one might state it by saying that thought, when it follows its own bent most completely and sets itself the task of thinking out the idea of an object that shall completely satisfy the demands of reason, may appear to be constructing a mere *ens rationis*, but in fact is never devoid of objective or ontological reference.

Anselm's argument, that in conceiving a perfect being we are conceiving a subject possessed of all positive predicates, including that of existence, so that to think of this is already to think of it as existing, is an argument open to objection on the logical ground that existence is not a predicate; but the substance of his thought survives all such objections, no less than it survives the baseless accusation that he was trying to argue from a mere thought to the existence of its object. He was careful to explain that his argument applied, not to thought in general, but only to the thought of one unique object, *id quo maius cogitari nequit*; the slightest acquaintance with writers like Boethius and Augustine is enough to show that he was deliberately referring to the absolute of neo-Platonic metaphysics; and in effect his argument amounts to this, that in the special case of metaphysical thinking the distinction between conceiving something and thinking it to exist is a distinction without a difference.

So understood, Anselm's argument was by no means either ignored or rejected in the later Middle Ages; his successors, if they criticized it at all, did so either because they found difficulties in its religious or theological implications, or else because they regarded its truth and certainty as being of an ultimate and fundamental sort that can only belong to some kind of axioms which precede and underlie all appeal to argument: a criticism whose validity cannot be here considered, since it belongs to a subject discussed in later chapters of this essay.

Of all the legacy of medieval thought, no part was more firmly seized upon than the Ontological Proof by those who laid the foundations of modern thought. Descartes, the acknowledged father of modern philosophy, made it the mainspring of his system; it was the Ontological Proof that gave him the power to move from the pin-point of momentary subjective consciousness to the infinite process of objective knowledge. Spinoza, who has been acclaimed as the purest representative of the realistic scientific spirit of the modern world, placed it even more prominently; and it remained the foundation-stone of every successive philosophy until Kant, whose attempt to refute it—perhaps the only occasion on which any one has rejected it who really understood what it meant—was rightly regarded by his successors as a symptom of that false subjectivism and consequent scepticism from which, in spite of heroic efforts, he never wholly freed himself. With Hegel's rejection of subjective idealism, the Ontological Proof took its place once more among the accepted principles of modern philosophy, and it has never again been seriously criticized.

6. Students of philosophy, when once they have learnt that the Proof is not to be dismissed as a

quibble, generally realize that it proves something, but find themselves perplexed to say what exactly this is. Clearly it does not prove the existence of whatever God happens to be believed in by the person who appeals to it. Between it and the articles of a particular positive creed there is no connexion, unless these articles can be deduced *a priori* from the idea of an *ens realissimum*. What it does prove is that essence involves existence, not always, but in one special case, the case of God in the metaphysical sense: the *Deus sive natura* of Spinoza, the Good of Plato, the Being of Aristotle: the object of metaphysical thought. But this means the object of philosophical thought in general; for metaphysics, even if it is regarded as only one among the philosophical sciences, is not unique in its objective reference or in its logical structure; all philosophical thought is of the same kind, and every philosophical science partakes of the nature of metaphysics, which is not a separate philosophical science but a special study of the existential aspect of that same subject-matter whose aspect as truth is studied by logic, and its aspect as goodness by ethics.

Reflection on the history of the Ontological Proof thus offers us a view of philosophy as a form of thought in which essence and existence, however clearly distinguished, are conceived as inseparable. On this view, unlike mathematics or empirical science, philosophy stands committed to maintaining that its subject-matter is no mere hypothesis, but something actually existing.

7. It may further be shown that this doctrine is deeply embedded in the whole fabric of the philosophical sciences as they actually exist; so that it is impossible to engage, however slightly, in the study of logic, for example, or ethics, without committing oneself to the view that one is studying a subject-matter that actually exists, and therefore aiming at a knowledge only expressible in categorical propositions. No proposed method of reforming these sciences, whether by changing their method or by redefining their subject-matter, will rid them of this characteristic.

Logic is concerned with thought as its subject-matter. It has a double character. On the one hand it is descriptive, and aims at giving an account of how we actually think; on the other it is normative, and aims at giving an account of the ideal of thought, the way in which we ought to think. If logic were merely descriptive, it would be a psychology of thinking; like all psychology, it would abstract from the distinction of thoughts into true and false, valid and invalid, and would consider them merely as events happening in the mind. In that case its purpose would be to provide a kind of anatomy or physiology of the understanding, and its aims, structure, and methods would conform on the whole to the pattern of empirical science. Throughout its long history logic has never taken up this position. It has no doubt ignored the distinction between true and false judgement, but it has done this only in pursuance of its conception of itself as the theory of inference; the distinction between valid and invalid reasoning it has never ignored.

But neither is logic merely normative. A purely normative science would expound a norm or ideal of what its subject-matter ought to be, but would commit itself to no assertion that this ideal was anywhere realized. If logic were a science of this kind, it would resemble the exact sciences; it would in fact either be, or be closely related to, mathematics. The reason why it can never conform to that pattern is that whereas in geometry, for example, the subject-matter is triangles, &c., and the body of the science consists of propositions about triangles, &c., in logic the subject-matter is propositions, and the body of the science consists of propositions about propositions. In geometry the body of the science is heterogeneous with its subject-matter; in logic they are homogeneous, and more than homogeneous, they are identical; for the propositions of which logic consists must conform to the rules which logic lays down, so that logic is actually about itself; not about itself exclusively, but at least incidentally about itself.

It follows that logic cannot be in substance merely hypothetical. Geometry can afford to be indifferent to the existence of its subject-matter; so long as it is free to suppose it, that is enough. But logic cannot share this indifference, because, by existing, it constitutes an actually existing subject-matter to itself. Thus, when we say 'all squares have their diagonals equal', we need not be either explicitly or implicitly asserting that any squares exist; but when we say 'all universal propositions distribute their subject', we are not only discussing universal propositions, we are also enunciating a universal proposition; we are producing an actual instance of the thing under discussion, and cannot discuss it without doing so. Consequently no such discussion can be indifferent to the existence of its own subject-matter; in other words, the propositions which constitute the body of logic cannot ever be in substance hypothetical. A logician who lays it down that all universal propositions are merely hypothetical is showing a true insight into the nature of science, but he is undermining the very possibility of logic; for his assertion cannot be true consistently with the fact of his asserting it.

Similarly with inference. Logic not only discusses, it also contains, reasoning; and if a logician could believe that no valid reasoning anywhere actually existed, he would merely be disbelieving his own logical theory. For logic has to provide not only a theory of its subject-matter, but in the same breath a theory of itself; it is an essential part of its proper task that it should consider not only how other kinds of thought proceed, and on what principles, but how and on what principles logic proceeds. If it had only to consider other kinds of thought, it could afford to deal with its subject-matter in a way either merely normative or merely descriptive; but towards itself it can only stand in an attitude that is both at once. It is obliged to produce, as constituent parts of itself, actual instances of thought which realize its own ideal of what thought should be.

Logic, therefore, stands committed to the principle of the Ontological Proof. Its subject-matter, namely thought, affords an instance of something which cannot be conceived except as actual, something whose essence involves existence.

8. Moral philosophy, by a different path, reaches the same goal. Like logic, it cannot be either merely descriptive or merely normative. Had it been merely descriptive, it would have contented itself with giving an account of the various ways in which people actually behave. This would have been a psychology or anthropology of conduct, in which no account could have been taken of moral ideas and the conformity, or lack of conformity, to them which action displays. There is a science of this kind, and it has its place in the system of the empirical sciences; but it is not moral philosophy.

Had it been merely normative, it would have set aside all question how people actually behave, and endeavoured to answer the question how they ought to behave. But people do not need, and would not tolerate, such guidance from moral theorists. To decide how he ought to behave is the task of the agent himself; a task in which the moral theorist can help, if he can, only because he too is a moral agent, and the moral agent in his degree already a moral theorist.

It would be better, combining a normative with a descriptive conception, to define moral philosophy as giving an account of how people think they ought to behave. Here the facts and the ideals of conduct are alike included in the subject-matter; but the ideals might seem to be reduced to a mere new kind or order of facts. To correct this, it must be borne in mind that the question how people think is not in any philosophical science separable from the question whether they think rightly or wrongly; and thus moral philosophy has to face the responsibility either of holding that people are always right when they think they ought to do some act, or of instituting some kind of comparison and criticism of moral judgements. In the first alternative, the view is taken that the moral ideal already exists as an ideal in the minds of all moral agents; in the second, that it partially so exists, and more completely as (with or without help from moral philosophy) they try to think out more clearly what they believe their duties to be. In either case, the science is both normative and descriptive; it describes, not action as opposed to ideas about action, but the moral consciousness; and this it is forced to describe as already being in some sense what it ought to be. This in turn will affect the account which it gives of action; for no theory of moral ideals is conceivable which does not admit that to some extent moral ideas affect action.

Quite apart, then, from any argument which might be directed to showing, perhaps legitimately, that the moral philosopher in describing virtue must himself, in his work as a thinker, display some at least of the virtues he describes—sincerity, truthfulness, perseverance, courage, and justice—it is clear that the moral ideal, which it is his business to conceive, cannot be conceived as a mere thought wholly divorced from existence. Here too the Ontological Proof holds good: the subject-matter of ethical thought must be conceived as something whose essence involves existence.

§ 3

9. Without considering cases drawn from other philosophical sciences, I may now venture to state generally that the body of any philosophical science consists of categorical propositions and not merely, as in the case of exact and empirical science, of hypothetical. This is not to deny that philosophical thought involves hypothetical elements. The hypothetical judgements of science, as we have seen, involve various kinds of categorical judgements as accessories or conditions of their substantive being; and conversely if the body of philosophical knowledge consists of categorical judgements it must at least be surrounded, as it were, by a scaffolding of hypotheticals; I mean that, in order to decide that a certain theory is true, our affirmation of this theory must be supported by considering what the consequences would have been, had any of the alternative theories been true. In this sense the working-out of conclusions from purely hypothetical premisses is a very necessary part of philosophical thinking, though a subsidiary part.

But it is not enough to say that in science the body of knowledge is hypothetical with subsidiary categorical elements, and vice versa in philosophy; for in philosophy the relation between the two elements is more intimate than that contrast would imply. Just as the principle of concrete affirmation lays it down that the negative element in a philosophical assertion, so far from being a separate judgement, is a determining factor which gives point and precision to the significance of the affirmation, so the hypothetical element, which I have described as a kind of scaffolding to the categorical body of thought, is really an integral part of that body itself, though a part subsidiary to the categorical. I need hardly add that the whole comprising these two parts is not an aggregate; for each is necessary to the other, and is what it is by virtue of its relation to the other.

10. This view of philosophy as categorical thinking, even apart from its agreement with the pronouncements of philosophers, its connexion with the argument of the Ontological Proof, and its verification in the actual procedure of the philosophical sciences, is a necessary consequence of the overlap of classes, and therefore follows from the hypothesis of the present essay. Categorical and hypothetical are two species of judgement; according to the hypothesis, therefore, in non-philosophical judgements they will constitute separate classes, so that the universal judgements forming the body of science can be purely hypothetical; in philosophical judgements they will overlap, so that those forming the body of philosophy cannot be merely hypothetical but must be at the same time categorical.

This, however, states the position too simply; and if the reader will bear with me I will correct it. The concept of judgement is already a philosophical concept, and therefore an overlap of its specific forms can never be wholly avoided. Even in science, therefore, the overlap exists; and this I have already recognized by showing that the purely hypothetical propositions forming the body of science involve certain categorical elements which are necessary to their being but form no part of their essence *qua* science; these are, as it were, a solid structure of facts and truths upon which the pliant body of scientific hypothesis leads a parasitic life. But in the case of philosophical judgements the overlap becomes peculiarly intimate; the categorical element is no longer something external to the hypothetical, even if necessary to it; both elements alike are of the essence of philosophy as such. As before, what we find here is a peculiar fusion of logical elements which elsewhere are found either separate or united in a relatively loose and external way. If it is asked whether the distinction is that between a closer and a looser union, or that between absolute union and absolute separation, I may perhaps reply that in principle that question has been answered in discussing the idea of a scale of forms.

11. A complete theory of knowledge would have to go much further at this point. It would have to consider not only the formal distinction of philosophy from science, but the relation of each to the other as substantive bodies of knowledge. It would have

to ask whether the hypothetical element in philosophy is identical with science itself, or whether it is something peculiar to philosophy; and whether the categorical skeleton upon which are supported the hypothetical tissues of scientific thought proper is wholly or partly identical with philosophy. It would also have to discuss the theory of history, and the relation between the categorical singular judgement which composes the body of historical thought and the categorical universal of philosophy. But for the purpose of this essay enough has been said about the logical relation of the judgement when it has been shown that the philosophical judgement is in essence and substance categorical.

VII

TWO SCEPTICAL POSITIONS

1. As in science and in history, so in philosophy the ideal of thought demands that no proposition be admitted into the body of knowledge except for sufficient reason, or, in logical terms, as the conclusion of an inference. The question must therefore be raised: by what special kind of reasoning or inference are the propositions of philosophy established?

There are persons who think that this question admits of no answer; who believe, that is, that no such thing as constructive philosophical reasoning is possible. Like most sceptics, they do not adopt this belief lightly; they are driven to it after serious thought, and their doubts deserve serious consideration. They agree in disclaiming, whether for themselves merely, or for their own generations, or for the entire body of human thinkers everywhere and always, any philosophical doctrine supported by constructive philosophical argument; but beyond this they differ. Some deny that they have any philosophical doctrine at all, and hold that philosophical reasoning is not constructive but critical, its function being solely to destroy false philosophies. Others claim to have a philosophical position, but think that the judgements that go to make it up are based not on philosophical arguments but on science or common sense.

§ 1

2. 'I do not know,' say the first of these, 'what the right answer to any philosophical question is; but I think there is work to be done in showing that the answers usually given are wrong. And I can prove that one answer is wrong without claiming to know that another is right; for my method is to examine the answers given by other people, and to show that they are self-contradictory. What is self-contradictory is, properly speaking, meaningless; what is meaningless cannot mean the truth; and therefore by this method I can preserve a purely critical attitude towards the philosophy of others, without having any philosophy of my own. As to that, I neither assert nor deny its possibility; I merely, for the present, suspend judgement and continue my work of criticism.'

A philosophy which defines its task in this way I propose to call a critical philosophy, meaning by that a philosophy which sets out to be critical as opposed to constructive. A critical attitude, in this sense, differs from the attitude of abstract negation described in the fifth chapter in the way in which inference differs from judgement: to negate a view is simply to assert its falsity, to criticize it is to give reasons for this assertion. In using the term critical here I am inevitably suggesting a comparison with the Critical Philosophy of Kant; but what I have to say on this subject must not be understood as directed to Kant's address; for criticism, in his view, was not the whole of his philosophy; it is directed rather at one of the various schools of thought which have divided Kant's inheritance.

3. The merits of such an attitude need no emphasis. But it has defects of two kinds. First, it betrays a defect of temper. It is characteristic of acute and accomplished thinkers, used to studying closely the work of great writers, who have become disheartened and inclined to dismiss all philosophical thought as futile. This failure of heart is bound up with a failure of sympathy towards the writers whom they criticize. To study a philosophy with the avowed intention, not of asking how adequately it deals with its subject-matter, but solely of looking for inconsistencies in its logical form, implies a withdrawal of interest from that which most interested the author, the subject-matter, and a consequent alienation of sympathy from him which makes it impossible to estimate his work fairly. Criticism of this kind will bear most hardly on writers who are genuinely grappling with the intricacies of a difficult problem, and, since the critic claims no knowledge of the subject-matter, they will get from him no credit for the insight which they have shown; it will be most lenient to those who, abandoning all attempt at profound or close study of the matter in hand, content themselves with a one-sided account of some partial aspect of it. Consequently criticism of this kind is not only based on a defective scale of values, but its judgements run grave risk of being inversely related to the merits of the authors judged; and even if that danger is averted its general temper,

instead of being sympathetic, as good criticism should be, can hardly escape being superficial and to some extent frivolous.

4. Defects of temper, I may be told, are irrelevant in philosophy, which, as the pursuit of truth, cares only for logical values, not moral. So be it. The philosopher I am criticizing is no less open to criticism in his logic. He asserts that he has no philosophical doctrine of his own; but this assertion is belied by his practice, which implies two things, each in effect a constructive philosophical position.

He has condemned the philosophies of other people for showing certain characteristics which, he thinks, are faults. This implies a conception of what a constructive philosophy should be, and the use of this conception as a standard by which to condemn existing philosophies. Now, the idea of a philosophy is itself a philosophical idea; and the critic who uses such an idea as a standard is under an obligation to state it and defend it against criticism.

He has also a conception of what philosophical criticism should be; and this is a standard whose claims he thinks he can and does satisfy in his own philosophical practice. But this again is a philosophical conception; and hence a philosophical critic is bound to give us his theory of philosophical criticism, and satisfy us by positive or constructive argument that his principles are sound and that his practice faithfully follows them.

Scepticism in this form, as in all its forms, is in reality a covert dogmatism; it contains positive theories of the nature, method, and limitations of philosophical thought, but disclaims their possession and conceals them from criticism. Hence it is both inconsistent, or false to its own professed principles, and—intentionally or unintentionally—dishonest, because applying to others a form of criticism which in its own case it will not admit.

§ 2

5. A second form of scepticism agrees with the first in holding that philosophy cannot establish positive or constructive positions; but holds that we are not on that account necessarily ignorant of the right answers to philosophical questions. These answers are supplied, it maintains, not by philosophical argument but by science and common sense.

For example: is there a material world? are there other minds beside my own? Yes; common sense tells me that these things are so; philosophical thinking is neither needed to convince me of them, nor able to demonstrate them, if I am so foolish as to doubt them or so disingenuous as to profess a doubt I cannot feel.

On the other hand, there are many questions, traditionally referred to philosophy for decision, which, because they cannot be decided by science or common sense, cannot be decided at all. Is there a God; shall we have a future life; what is the general nature of the universe as a whole? Because we do not know the answers to these questions independently of philosophizing, philosophy cannot give them.

What, then, is left for philosophy to do? It has no longer, as on the critical view, the function of controverting error; for example, it does not demolish the false view that duty is merely expediency and leave us ignorant indeed but free from delusions; for, according to this view, we know what duty is, and always did know; if any one asks what it is, we can reply 'it is what you and I and every one know it to be'. Nothing is left for philosophy except the task of analysing the knowledge we already possess: taking the propositions which are given by science and common sense, and revealing their logical structure or 'showing what exactly we mean when we say', for example, that there is a material world.

6. Like the other, this form of scepticism is the fruit of much philosophical learning and labour; both alike are historical products of a study of the *Critique of Pure Reason* and the problems of which it is the classical discussion; both are worthy of respect and, as we shall see, within limits true. But the analytic view is hardly more defensible than the critical.

If a person holding a view of this type were asked to state his philosophical position, he would probably begin by stating a series of propositions belonging to the sphere of common sense, which some philosophers have, wrongly as he thinks, questioned or denied.[1] But the task of philosophy, on this view,

[1] I think that Professor G. E. Moore takes this line in his 'Defence of Common Sense' (*Contemporary British Philosophy*, vol. ii, pp. 193 seqq.); for here, on pp. 195–6, he states a proposi-

is to analyse such propositions as these; and consequently a philosopher holding this view would presumably describe as part of his philosophical position not only the data of analysis, the propositions of common sense, such as 'this is a human hand', but the results of analysis, such propositions as 'there is a thing, and only one thing, of which it is true both that it is a human hand and that this surface is a part of its surface'. But the analytic view of philosophy implies a third class of propositions: neither the data of analysis (the common-sense propositions to be analysed), nor its results (the propositions into which these are resolved), but the principles according to which it proceeds; some of them logical, such as that a complex proposition can be divided up into two or more simple ones, some metaphysical, such as (to take one involved in the above instance) that sense-data are not mental entities which somehow represent physical objects, but are actually parts of physical objects.

The analytic philosopher, invited to state his philosophical position, would perhaps include in the statement propositions of all these three classes. But, on such a view of philosophy, it is not quite clear

tion which on p. 207 he calls the first point in his philosophical position; and the gist of this proposition, which I venture to abbreviate—it is nearly 200 words long—is as follows: Many other human beings beside myself have frequently known, *mutatis mutandis*, what I know when I say such things as, I am a human being, or, the mantelpiece is nearer to me than the bookcase. I suppose Professor Moore to think that this proposition is vouched for by common sense.

that data, results, and principles have an equal right to be included. The data of analysis are only the subject-matter upon which philosophical thought exercises itself, as logic may exercise itself on propositions made (for example) by a botanist. That all oaks are dicotyledonous is not a part of logical theory; the logician is not, as a logician, called upon either to assert it or deny it. He merely studies its logical structure. Hence, if the philosopher's task is neither to attack nor to defend the statements of common sense, but only to analyse them, such a statement as 'there are other human beings with experiences like my own' cannot be a part of his philosophical position; it is only an example of the things about which he philosophizes; and to think of it as an element in his philosophical position is to relapse into that very view of philosophy as criticizing or corroborating common sense against which this theory is expressly in revolt.

The results of analysis would seem to be in the same case. For the analysis of a common-sense proposition states what exactly that proposition means; and if the datum of analysis is a common-sense proposition, its result, being identical with it in meaning, is a common-sense proposition also.

The one class of propositions which beyond any doubt ought to be included in the analytic philosopher's statement of his position is that which comprises the principles on which analysis proceeds. These principles constitute a theory concerning the nature and method of philosophy; this is a philosophical theory, and a constructive one; and, therefore, whatever else the analytical philosopher ought to tell us when asked to state his philosophical position, it is clear that his first duty is to expound these. Yet he, like the critical philosopher, not only neglects this duty but makes a merit of neglecting it and asserting that he has no constructive or systematic theory of his own.

7. That exponents of this view ought not to neglect the duty of examining or even stating their own principles is admitted by some of themselves. Dr. L. S. Stebbing, in a recent paper on 'The Method of Analysis in Metaphysics' (*Proceedings of the Aristotelian Society*, 1932–3, pp. 65–94), reminds us that the analytic method has been much used by well-known philosophers in this country for over twenty years, but that none of them has 'seen fit to raise' the questions upon what presuppositions it rests and whether they can be justified (p. 75). In raising these questions Dr. Stebbing claims (and justly, so far as my acquaintance with the previous literature goes) to be breaking new ground. But although in the paper quoted there is an attempt to state these presuppositions, it is admitted that 'nearly all the great philosophers of the past' have implicitly denied them (p. 66), and no attempt is made to rebut these implicit denials or to offer the smallest reason why the assumptions should be granted. It is even admitted that 'so far from being certainly justified, [they] are not even very plausible' (p. 92) and the strongest argument in favour of any is that 'I see no reasons against it'.

Here again, therefore, the conclusion must be that analytical philosophy, like critical philosophy, is a method resting on principles; that these principles constitute or imply a constructive philosophical position, and that the one indisputably philosophical task which exponents of the analytic method have imposed upon themselves is the task of expounding and justifying this position. But a great part of the attraction of the analytic method lies in its claim to have done away with the old idea of constructive philosophy; and the only comment which can now be made on that claim is that analytic philosophy does indeed involve a constructive philosophical doctrine, but, true to its character as a form of scepticism, declines the task of stating it.

8. It may be replied that these principles, even if never openly stated and defended against criticism, are nevertheless, in the working of the analytic method, justified by their results. But, in the first place, the exponents of that method are eager to assure us that its results are very modest: that it can never solve any of the problems which have been in the past—and by most people are in the present—regarded as the main problems of philosophy: that, in short, the prospect opened by the method 'seems at first sight disappointing' (Russell, *Our Knowledge of the External World*, p. 27). And secondly, our only reason for accepting these results is that we accept the method which yields them. An argument to persuade us that people think or act in certain ways can be tested *a posteriori*; if they do so act or think, the argument

is to that extent confirmed. But an argument to persuade us that when we say 'this is a human hand' we mean 'there is a thing, and only one thing, of which it is true both that it is a human hand and that this surface is a part of its surface' is an argument which points to no new fact and therefore cannot be verified by any *a posteriori* test.

9. Both these sceptical theories, therefore, break down under examination, and both for the same reason. Each disclaims a constructive philosophy; each claims to possess, not a body of doctrine, but only a method: not a method of reaching positive philosophical conclusions, but a method of doing something else—in the one case, of demolishing false philosophies, in the other, of deciding what exactly we mean when we make a statement. They both fail to recognize that methods imply principles, and systematic methods, systematic principles; and that their professed scepticism is merely a veiled claim to exempt these principles from criticism or even from explicit statement, while assuming their truth and sufficiency. While this state of things continues, it cannot be allowed that the critical or analytic philosopher, however much we may value him as a commentator or critic of the philosophy of others, has even begun the task of formulating a philosophical position or programme of his own.

10. These two theories of the scope and method of philosophy have been examined on their merits, and shown to transgress the rules laid down by themselves; but they might have been rejected after

a much shorter examination. Each is in conflict with the first principle of philosophical method whose statement was the task of this essay's second chapter; and had the writer been willing to presume on the reader's assent to that principle, the criticism would have gone as follows.

The critical view assumes that an argument can be destructive without being constructive. This implies that constructive and destructive arguments are two species of a genus; and in that case our first principle tells us that in philosophy they will overlap, and may overlap to any extent; in other words, a philosopher developing a purely destructive argument is sure to be committing himself, consciously or unconsciously, to a constructive position, and his only choice is whether this position shall be explicitly and critically developed or surreptitiously assumed.

The analytical view assumes that there is not only a distinction, which would be willingly conceded, but a difference between knowing that this is a table and knowing what I mean when I say that it is a table. Asserting a proposition and analysing it are species of a genus which is defined[1] as 'the attitude adopted towards' the proposition. But if in the case of philosophy the species of a genus overlap, asserting and analysing, however distinct, cannot in

[1] W. E. Johnson, *Logic*, i. 6. Johnson does not there include analysing among the attitudes he enumerates, but I imagine that the text fairly represents the position as conceived by the school of thought I am discussing.

philosophy be separated; and a philosopher, invited to affirm or deny a given proposition, retains the right to say 'I cannot tell whether I think this proposition true or false until I understand what it means'. This is how traditional philosophy has always replied to invitations of this kind; and the whole contention of the analytic school is that, in so replying, it has been the victim of a confusion between assertion and analysis. It must by now be clear that the confusion exists solely in the mind of the analytic philosopher who is arguing that, because the traditional philosopher says 'I cannot do *A* without doing *B*', he is failing to distinguish *A* and *B*, when in reality he is distinguishing them and refusing to separate them. In short, the traditional procedure is sound, and the advocate of analysis is not so much attempting to reform philosophical method as quarrelling with it for being philosophical.

This method of criticism has not been adopted, because although the reader, by the terms of our compact made in the second chapter, has agreed to accept these principles as hypotheses and to see where they lead us, he has a right to demand that on such a journey our position should be checked from time to time by asking how the conclusions derived from the original assumptions tally with results otherwise obtained. It is easy to begin an argument with assumptions containing some small error which, as the argument proceeds, multiplies itself at every step; and it is an elementary precaution against this danger, to demand that the initial assumption shall be constantly verified by such cross-reference. This principle is especially important in philosophical argument because, as the preceding chapter has contended, philosophical thought knows no mere assumptions, and therefore cannot proceed on the principle that the truth or falsity of its initial hypotheses is a matter of indifference.

It was therefore desirable to show that these two sceptical positions were not only to be condemned as inconsistent with our agreed hypothesis, but could be proved fallacious by their own standards. Such verification of our original assumption may encourage the reader to persevere in the task of working out its consequences, and also foreshadows the view of philosophical reasoning which will be stated in the following chapter. When that has been done, we shall see that the two theories criticized in this chapter are both in a sense justified as expressing some part of the truth, although by denying the rest they reduce this partial truth to error.

VIII
DEDUCTION AND INDUCTION

§ 1

1. IN considering the nature of philosophical inference it is convenient to begin by asking 'is it deductive or inductive?' This implies comparing it with the deductive reasoning of exact science and the inductive reasoning of empirical; and this I shall try to do, subject to the warning given in the first chapter (§ 2. 6) that my business is not to ask how reasoning is actually done in exact or empirical science, but how it ought to be done in philosophy.

Three things can be distinguished in all inference: the data from which we argue, the principles according to which we argue, and the conclusions to which we argue. In exact science the data are suppositions: for example, that *ABC* is a right-angled triangle. The principles are the so-called axioms: for example, that if equals be added to equals the sums will be equal. The conclusions are inferred in the sense of being demonstrated, that is, shown to follow with perfect logical rigour from the data according to the principles.

2. The axioms necessary to an exact science consist, it would seem, of two kinds. First, there are axioms belonging properly not to the body of that science, but to logic: these are the principles according to which demonstration as such must always

proceed. Secondly, there are others belonging to the science itself: in Euclid, for example, that two straight lines cannot enclose a space.

The first or logical axioms are necessary to science, but they are not part of science. They are necessary to it in the sense that unless they were true the science could not take a single step in advance; so that although they may be called its presuppositions, they are not mere suppositions. They are not part of it because they belong to logic, and the success of the science which presupposes them does not in turn confirm them. To confirm or to question them is the business of logic. The argument of exact science moves from these axioms in an irreversible direction, and hangs with its whole weight from them as from a fixed point.

The second or special axioms form part of the science, but a peculiar part. According to the older view of exact science, they are known to be true, but have the character—admittedly anomalous in an exact science—of not requiring demonstration. They are self-evident, or known to be true without being proved; not only is it possible to see their truth in this way (for demonstrable truths can sometimes be seen, by a rather mysterious kind of intuition, to be necessarily true, although we can at the moment see no proof of them) but it is the only way in which their truth can be seen; they do not admit of any demonstration whatever. Thus the certainly true propositions forming the body of an exact science fall into two classes:

the indemonstrable, or special axioms, and the demonstrable, or conclusions.

The main lines of this view are not, for our purposes, affected if it is maintained that the special axioms are not known to be true, but only assumed. The logical axioms cannot be merely assumed, for (as was shown in the sixth chapter) a philosophical proposition must always be categorical; we cannot think as if the principles of thinking were true, for if they were not true we should not be thinking. But the special axioms may be regarded as mere assumptions; and in that case we shall have to say that the entire body of the science consists of assumptions, but that these fall into two classes: primary or fundamental assumptions, the so-called special axioms, and secondary or derivative assumptions, the so-called conclusions.

3. In either case the argument has a property which I shall describe by saying that it is irreversible. The conclusions are logically dependent on the axioms; there is no reciprocal dependence of the axioms on the conclusions: our attitude towards the axioms is in no way affected by the discovery that they lead to these particular results; on the contrary, it is only because we accept the axioms first, that we accept the conclusions to which they lead.

This irreversibility is a necessary attribute of exact science: it can only argue forwards, from principles to conclusions, and can never turn round and argue backwards, from conclusions to principles, whether these are understood as special principles peculiar to itself and forming part of its own body, or general principles belonging to the body of logic. To guard against a misunderstanding, it may be remarked that though the argument of an exact science can never be reversible in respect of its principles, it may be and generally is reversible in respect of its data; given the axioms, which are equally necessary in both cases, we can argue either that because the sides are equal the angles at the base are equal, or that because the angles at the base are equal the sides are equal.

§ 2

4. In its demand for close and cogent reasoning, philosophy resembles exact science. Each alike works on the principle that no conclusions may be asserted for which valid and sufficient reason cannot be given. It is natural, therefore, that in its inferential methods philosophy should present certain analogies with mathematics; but it does not follow that the methods are, or ever can be, identical at every point.

One necessary difference is that the division of axioms into those belonging to the science in question, and those belonging to logic, disappears. Logic is a branch of philosophy, and not a branch separable from the others; even if a person investigating a problem in ethics could afford to say 'this point in my problem I can entirely leave on one side, for it is a logical point, not an ethical one', the question would merely be deferred, for the philosopher as such is obliged to study logic sooner or later. Consequently, whereas other sciences can neglect their own logical presuppositions, philosophy cannot; and therefore it has not two kinds of axioms, but only one, namely the kind that form a part of its own body.

5. But there is a second difference. The axioms of philosophy, because they are philosophical propositions, must be categorically asserted; they cannot be mere assumptions. This would seem to imply that they are self-evident propositions, forming the first principles of an irreversible deductive system of thought. Is such a view tenable?

If any one has ever held it, one would expect to find it in the works of the great mathematician-philosophers of the seventeenth century; for probably no one has ever had such motives or such qualifications for introducing mathematical methods into philosophy as Descartes and his successors.

6. When Descartes, dissatisfied with the results of all systematic thinking before his own day, resolved to begin again from the beginning, he did not explicitly distinguish the case of philosophy from that of the other sciences; and, as has been already pointed out in the first chapter, the method on which he undertook to work in the future was to be applied to all three branches of knowledge—metaphysics, natural science, and mathematics—without distinction, although it was admittedly a method derived from mathematics. Ostensibly, therefore, Descartes would seem an example, for good or ill,

of mathematical method applied to philosophy. But when we forget his theory of method and turn to his practice, we find that, when actually engaged in philosophical work, Descartes was far too good a philosopher to neglect the necessary differences between philosophical and mathematical reasoning.

His first principle, 'I think, therefore I am', is neither a self-evident truth nor an assumption. Although a starting-point for all his metaphysical reasoning, it is actually established, in the passage where he first enunciates it, by a proof; and it appears on analysis that this is a proof of the peculiar kind to which Kant was later to give the name of a transcendental deduction. Convinced that a great part of our fancied knowledge is error, Descartes has set himself the task of challenging it in detail, and doubting everything dubitable. 'I soon observed', he continues, 'that, determined as I was to think everything false, it was absolutely necessary that I who thought this should be something.'[1]

In Kantian language, the principle *cogito ergo sum* is in this passage transcendentally deduced, that is, shown to be the condition on which experience as it actually exists, in this case the experience of systematic doubt, is alone possible.[2] If I did not exist as

[1] *Discours de la Méthode*, *quatrième partie*, *ad init.* 'Mais aussitôt après je pris garde que, pendant que je voulais ainsi penser que tout était faux, il fallait nécessairement que moi qui le pensais fusse quelque chose.'

[2] Cf., e.g., *Kritik d. r. Vernunft*, *Trans. Anal.*, ch. ii, § 14, 'Übergang zur trans. Ded. der Kat.', A 93, B 126: 'folglich wird die objektive Gültigkeit der Kategorien, als Begriffe a

a thinking being, I could not doubt. Even doubt of my own existence is therefore a guarantee of my existence. Whatever Descartes's explicit theory of philosophical method may have been, here in practice he shows an entirely just sense of the difference between that and mathematical.

It would be doing Descartes an injustice to suggest that he himself was blind to this fact. His explicit programme, as laid down in the *Discours*, no doubt recognized only one method *pour bien conduire sa raison et chercher la vérité dans les sciences*, and contained no hint that there might be a peculiar method appropriate to the peculiar problems of philosophical thought. A reader would naturally infer that his intention was to assimilate the method of philosophy in every particular to that of mathematics ; but when this inference was actually drawn, and a correspondent, some years later, invited him to state his views on certain metaphysical questions *selon la méthode des géomètres, en laquelle vous êtes si bien versé*, Descartes answered by acceding to the request, and thus providing Spinoza with his model for a body of

priori, darauf beruhen, dass durch sie allein Erfahrung (der Form des Denkens nach) möglich sei.' The same method applies to principles : A 148–9, B 188 : 'Grundsätze a priori führen diesen Namen nicht bloss deswegen, weil sie die Gründe anderer Urteile in sich enthalten (i.e. are starting-points for reasoning) sondern auch weil sie selbst nicht in höheren und allgemeineren Erkenntnissen gegründet sind (i.e. cannot be deductively demonstrated). Diese Eigenschaft überhebt sie doch nicht allemal eines Beweises . . . (this necessary proof is obtained) aus den subjektiven Quellen der Möglichkeit einer Erkenntnis des Gegenstandes überhaupt.

philosophical doctrine *ordine geometrico demonstrata*, but at the same time remarking that in one way the method is ill suited to metaphysics, where, quite otherwise than in mathematics, 'the chief difficulty is to conceive the first notions clearly and distinctly'.[1]

7. The full magnitude of that difficulty may not have been realized until Kant awoke from his dogmatic slumber; but it was never wholly overlooked by the great successors of Descartes, who always interpreted his precepts in the light of his practice. The 'geometrical method' of Spinoza differs from the method of geometry in the very point to which Descartes had called his correspondent's attention. As if to emphasize his own recognition of this point, Spinoza has packed the whole of Anselm's Ontological Proof, as restated by Descartes, into what purports to be his 'first definition', the opening sentence of the *Ethics*. When he writes: 'By *cause of itself* I understand that whose essence involves existence, and whose nature cannot be conceived except as existing,'[2] he is doing something very different from defining his terms *more geometrico*. His statement is not a definition but a theorem: a philosophical position, and, as he well knew, an arguable and argued position.

Leibniz does the same. In the epigrammatic

[1] *Deuxièmes objections* (*Œuvres*, ed. Simon, p. 160); *Réponses aux deuxièmes objections* (ibid., p. 182).

[2] *Ethics*, part I, def. 1. 'Per *causam sui* intelligo id cuius essentia involvit existentiam, sive id cuius natura non potest concipi nisi existens.'

brevity of the *Monadology* he begins with two clauses having the appearance of a definition and an axiom, and together stating the conception of an unextended and indivisible substance;[1] but Leibniz knew, and trusted his readers to remember, that this was a conception which raised many of the most ancient and disputed problems in philosophy, and that he, like Spinoza, was beginning his treatise not by defining his terms like a mathematician but by laying down a whole metaphysical system in a nutshell, and not by stating a self-evident axiom but by affirming a highly controversial theorem.

8. When, therefore, Kant laid it down that philosophy could contain no axioms, and that its first principles required proof, but proof of a special kind; when he attacked in principle and in detail the use of mathematical methods in philosophy, and concluded that they could lead to nothing but 'houses of cards'[2]; when Hegel, following Kant's lead, pointed out that philosophy was in the peculiar position of being obliged to justify its own starting-point; those contentions were not new: they were familiar to the great mathematical philosophers of

[1] '(1) La Monade, dont nous parlons ici, n'est autre chose qu'une substance simple qui entre dans les composés; simple, c'est-à-dire sans parties.

'(2) Et il faut qu'il y ait des substances simples, puisqu'il y a des composés; car le composé n'est autre chose qu'un amas ou *aggregatum* des simples.'

[2] *K.R.V.* A 727, B 755. 'Ich werde . . . zeigen . . . dass der Messkünstler, nach seiner Methode, in der Philosophie nichts als Kartengebäude zustande bringe.'

the seventeenth century, as they have always been to all competent philosophers; and if in their actual practice the Kantians to some extent departed from the method used by the Cartesians, taking more pains to avoid the dangers of a too close assimilation of philosophical thought to mathematical, they were only insisting on differences which the Cartesians, though they may have overlooked them in theory, had never wholly ignored, even though they may have missed some of their implications, in practice.

§ 3

9. But what can be meant by saying that philosophy must justify its own starting-point? Plainly it cannot mean that, before the work of substantive philosophy can begin, there must be a preliminary philosophy charged with the task of justifying its principles. That would be to support the world on an elephant, and the elephant on a tortoise: a procedure which, as Kant came to see, is not adequately explained by calling the elephant Metaphysics and the tortoise a Critical or Transcendental Propaedeutic. If the first principles of philosophy are to be justified, they must be justified by that philosophy itself.

This can be done only if the arguments of philosophy, instead of having an irreversible direction from principles to conclusions, have a reversible one, the principles establishing the conclusions and the conclusions reciprocally establishing the principles. But an argument of this kind, in which A rests on B and B rests reciprocally on A, is a vicious circle. Are we to conclude that philosophy is in the dilemma of either renouncing this characteristic function and conforming to the irreversible pattern of exact science, or else losing all cogency in a circular argument?

10. The solution of the dilemma lies in a feature of philosophical thought to which I have already referred more than once: the Socratic principle that philosophical reasoning leads to no conclusions which we did not in some sense know already. Every school of philosophical thought has accepted this principle, recognizing that philosophy does not, like exact or empirical science, bring us to know things of which we were simply ignorant, but brings us to know in a different way things which we already knew in some way; and indeed it follows from our own hypothesis; for if the species of a philosophical genus overlap, the distinction between the known and the unknown, which in a non-philosophical subject-matter involves a difference between two mutually exclusive classes of truths, in a philosophical subject-matter implies that we may both know and not know the same thing; a paradox which disappears in the light of the notion of a scale of forms of knowledge, where coming to know means coming to know in a different and better way.

Establishing a proposition in philosophy, then, means not transferring it from the class of things unknown to the class of things known, but making it known in a different and better way. For example, it is a relatively bad way of knowing a thing if we merely observe that it is so but do not understand why it is so; a better way of knowing it would be by observation and understanding together; and if by seeing certain facts in the light of certain principles we come to understand the facts and at the same time to have visible confirmation of the principles, this is a gain to our knowledge both of the principles and of the facts.

11. Here philosophical thought shows a contrast with that of the exact sciences. Our knowledge that the square on the hypotenuse is equal to the sum of the squares on the other two sides depends (I speak for myself) on the proof. There are cases, as I have already remarked, in which we intuitively apprehend the conclusion without any proof; but normally the proof is our only source of assurance that the conclusion is true. In philosophy this is not so; we know this normally without any proof at all; and the service which the proof does for us is not to assure us that it is so, but to show us why it is so, and thus enable us to know it better.

Even the most ostentatiously deductive philosophical system, therefore, for example that of Spinoza, can never be deductive in the sense in which geometry is deductive. Spinoza did not wait for the knowledge that 'he will be rejoiced who imagines what he hates to be destroyed' until he had constructed the proof given in his *Ethics* (III, prop. xx). On the contrary, he knew that, and perhaps all the other substantive propositions contained in the *Ethics*, before he ever conceived the idea of welding them into a system, or inventing proofs for them derived from a small number of first principles. The effect of constructing his ethical system, and this is true of philosophical systems in general, is to exhibit as a reasoned and ordered whole of interconnected knowledge what was already in substance known before the work of philosophizing began.

12. If philosophy differs from exact science in this way—the anticipation, as we may call it, of its conclusions by an experience that possesses them in substance before its reasoning begins—other differences will follow: the chief being that in philosophy the conclusions can be checked by comparing them with these anticipations, and that by this checking the principles at work in the reasoning can be verified. If this is so, the direction of the argument in respect of principles and conclusions is reversible, each being established by appeal to the other; but this is not a vicious circle, because the word established here means raised to a higher grade of knowledge: what was a mere observation is now not merely observed but understood; what was a merely abstract principle is verified by appeal to facts.

This conception of philosophy, as reaffirming a knowledge already possessed in substance before we began to philosophize, raises certain difficulties, and requires certain modifications and developments before it can be regarded as reasonably secure; but in the meantime its chief implication for the theory of inferential method in philosophy may be summarized as follows.

If the substance of philosophical knowledge is known to us, however dimly and confusedly, before philosophical reasoning begins, the purpose of that reasoning can only be to present it in a new form; and this will be a reasoned form, that is, the form of a system constructed according to certain principles. The philosopher who unfolds such a system is not spinning a web of ideas from the recesses of his own mind; he is expressing the results of his own experience and that of other people in a reasoned and orderly shape; and at every step in his argument, instead of asking one question only, as in exact science, namely 'What follows from the premisses?' he has to ask another as well: 'Does that conclusion agree with what we find in actual experience?' This test is therefore an essential part of philosophical reasoning, and any argument whose conclusion cannot be subjected to it is philosophically defective.

§ 4

13. This has taken us a long way from the conception of philosophy as a deductive science. As we now see it, the argument of a philosopher no longer hangs with its whole weight on the starting-point, it is supported throughout its texture by cross-references to experience. Is it, then, in the last resort, based on facts? Is philosophy nothing but a theory based on observation and experience, in short, an empirical science? In order to answer this question, we must consider what is meant by inference in empirical science.

Inductive reasoning seeks to establish universal propositions through an examination of individual facts. These facts are the data; the universal propositions are the conclusions; and there are also principles according to which the argument proceeds. The data are empirically known by perception or the historical record of perception in the past. The conclusion, at the beginning of the process, must already be present in the form of an hypothesis, to be tested by bringing it into relation with the data. At first it is put forward merely as a possibility; the aim of the process is to convert it into a probability, the more probable the better. It may become so highly probable as to be, for practical purposes, a certainty; but there is a line separating even the highest probability from certainty in the proper sense of that word, and this line the hypotheses of inductive reasoning can never cross. This answers the question what, in empirical science, is meant by the word establish; it means, to establish as probable.

The data, on the contrary, begin by being certain, and never become anything else. The inductive process adds nothing to this certainty, and takes nothing away from it: it rests entirely on observation. It is true that errors of observation occur, and that a conflict between a supposed observation and an established induction may lead us to correct such an error; but if the conflict persists there can be no question which must give way to the other. The business of the induction is to conform with the facts; they in no sense depend upon it, it depends upon them.

14. The principles of induction, like those of exact science, are of two kinds. Some of them are purely logical principles, which begin by being certain and can never become either more or less so as induction proceeds. Others, when we come to consider them, prove to be not only assumptions but assumptions having little or no inherent plausibility; the most we can say for them is that they are not known to be untrue, and that it is expedient to assume them. Of these two kinds of principles, the first are logically presupposed by all induction whatever; they therefore cannot be established by inductive reasoning. Nor, in any case, could an inductive argument suffice to establish them; for being logical principles they must be categorically affirmed, and, as we have seen, the conclusions of induction are never more than probable.

The second kind of principles (for instance, that the future will probably resemble the past, or the known the unknown) are necessary assumptions if we are ever going to argue, as in inductive thinking we always do, that because some S is P therefore probably all S is P. But these principles are in no sense confirmed by the successful conduct of the arguments based on them. Unless we assumed them, we could never conduct arguments of this kind at all; but however long and however successfully we go on conducting arguments of this kind, we always know that these assumptions are assumptions and nothing more. What is increased by the success of our inductive inquiries is not the probability of such principles as that the future will resemble the past, but the probability of such hypotheses as that fermentation is due to micro-organisms. The principles never appear as conclusions, even in the modified sense in which conclusions exist in inductive thinking.

The logical movement of inductive thought is therefore irreversible in the same sense as that of exact science. The principles on which induction rests receive in return no support from the inductive process itself. Either they are certain from beginning to end, or from beginning to end they are mere assumptions.

The process of thought in exact science, though irreversible as regards its principles, may be reversible as regards its data (*supra*, § 1. 3 *ad fin.*). In this respect, inductive argument is not reversible; for its data are what they are because they enjoy the status of facts vouched for by perception; and although we can infer the existence of an unobserved fact from reasons inductively established by the study of similar facts, we only infer it (where to infer, as always in the context of inductive thought, means to establish as probable) and do not perceive it.

15. Although there is a resemblance, therefore, between the initial knowledge concerning the subject-matter of philosophy which we possess before we begin to philosophize, and the data of fact established by observation and experiment which we

possess at the outset of an inductive inquiry, there are important differences between the two things.

In philosophy the initial knowledge forms the substance of the final knowledge, the material out of which the system is constructed. The very same proposition which at first we knew to be true is reaffirmed with proofs in the body of the system. In empirical science the initial knowledge is not the material out of which, but the basis on which, the theory is built; thus the theory of cyclones does not require for its statement an exposition of the individual barometric or other observations on which it depends.

Secondly, in empirical science the initial knowledge consists of individual facts; but in philosophy, since the initial knowledge is homogeneous with the conclusions—otherwise the conclusions could not be the initial knowledge raised to a higher grade—and since the conclusions are universal propositions, the initial knowledge also must consist of universal propositions. The data of philosophy are thus never mere facts in the sense of individual events, individual objects, individual actions or the like; they are always universal; for example, in the case taken from Spinoza, the knowledge we ascribed to him before he began the work of systematic philosophizing was not the individual fact 'So-and-so, who hates such and such a thing, and imagines it to be destroyed, is pleased', but the universal proposition 'every one in these circumstances is pleased'.

Thirdly, the data of empirical science, as is natural

seeing that they are individual facts, are apprehended by perception; but the data of philosophy, if they are universal propositions, cannot be apprehended in that way; they must be grasped by something in the nature of what we call, as distinct from perceiving, thinking. If therefore we say that the initial knowledge on which philosophy rests as its data is arrived at by way of experience, we must add that the term experience in this case carries a special meaning: not the experience of a perceiver, but the experience of a thinker.

16. Thus the initial knowledge or datum in philosophy is very different from what it is in empirical science: different in its relation to the process of reasoning, different in its own constitution, different in the way in which we come to possess it. But the differences do not end here. That which it undergoes, as our thought proceeds, differs also.

In empirical science we begin by perceiving that the facts are so, and go on by forming a theory as to why they are so; but in adding this new theory to the old facts we do not come to know the facts in a different way, we only come to have something new in our minds—a new opinion, for it is not strictly knowledge, since it is never quite certain—alongside the old knowledge. The process is a special kind of accumulation. But in philosophy the knowledge (that word is applicable here) why things are so makes a difference to the knowledge that they are so. The new knowledge imparts a new quality to the old; in seeing why things are thus, we are not merely adding one piece of knowledge to another, we are coming to know the old better. Our knowledge is not simply accumulating, it is developing; it is improving as well as increasing; it is widening and strengthening itself at once.

17. There is consequently a parallel difference in the result of the process, the conclusion which the argument establishes. In the case of empirical science this is something new, something different from the data and added to them; in the case of philosophy it is the data themselves, developed into a new and more rational form. In empirical science, the outcome of an inductive process is an hypothesis standing, somewhat nebulously, outside the facts on which it depends, like the shadow of a mountain cast on a cloud; in philosophy, the theory that emerges from consideration of the facts is no mere hypothesis, it is the facts themselves more thoroughly understood, the two things are related somewhat as a mountain seen by itself is related to the same mountain seen in its place in the mountain-mass to which it belongs.

§ 5

18. To say that the conclusions of philosophy must be checked by appeal to experience, therefore, is valuable if it is merely intended as an indication of the way in which philosophical reasoning differs from that of the exact sciences; but it is misleading if it is taken as implying that the relation between theory and experience in philosophy resembles that which obtains in empirical science. In philosophy

there is a continuity between the experience and the theory; the theory is nothing but the experience itself, with its universality further insisted upon, its latent connexions and contradictions brought into the light of consciousness. Experience is already developing into theory, and theory is still experience; if theory must be checked by appeal to experience, experience in its turn can be supplemented by deduction from theory, and philosophers have been known to argue themselves into regions of experience where, except as philosophers, they have never travelled. But even that statement tends to over-emphasize the separation between theory and fact, which in philosophy is no separation at all, but only a distinction of the kind investigated in the third chapter, between specific developments of the same genus—philosophical knowledge—articulated in a scale of forms.

19. Accordingly when we distinguish, as we did in the case of Spinoza, the knowledge that a man has concerning moral questions before he begins to philosophize from the ordered system into which this knowledge is converted by philosophizing, the supposedly non-philosophical or pre-philosophical knowledge from which this process began is only in a relative sense non-philosophical. It is less philosophical than that into which it develops, but it is not strictly or absolutely non-philosophical; if we call it so, we are using the term only as we use the term illogical of an unsound argument, meaning not that there is no logic in it, but that there is not

enough, and that this defect impairs what logic there is. So, before people begin to do what we generally call philosophizing, the knowledge which they already possess is already full of philosophical elements; it is not at the zero end of the scale, for there is no zero end; it is, to say the least, at unity.

20. This gives a fresh meaning to the relation between the 'conclusions' of philosophical thinking and the 'experience' on which they are based, and by appeal to which they are checked. These two phrases are names for any two successive stages in the scale of forms of philosophical knowledge. What is called experience may be any stage in this scale; in itself, as all human experience must be, permeated through and through by philosophical elements; but relatively crude and irrational as compared with the next stage above it, in which these philosophical elements are more fully developed.

To say that theory must be checked by appeal to experience, therefore, seems like saying that the more rational must prove its rationality by conforming to the less rational, which seems like appealing from Philip sober to Philip drunk. But what is asked of the higher is not simply that it should agree with the lower, but rather that it should explain it: perpetuate its substance in a new form, related to the old somewhat as a fact *plus* the reasons for it is related to the bare fact. Consequently, when we ask whether a moral theory tallies with moral experience we are asking whether the theory makes intelligible the moral experience which we actually possess.

21. At every stage in the scale, there is a datum or body of experience, the stage that has actually been reached; and there is a problem, the task of explaining this experience by constructing a theory of it, which is nothing but the same experience raised by intenser thought to a higher level of rationality. The accomplishment of this task is only the continuation of a process already begun; it was only by thinking that we reached the point at which we stand, for the experience upon which we philosophize is already a rational experience; so our reason for going on is that we already stand committed to the task. But the new and intenser thinking must be thinking of a new kind; new principles are appearing in it, and these give a criterion by which the principles involved in the last step are superseded. Thus the stage last reached, regarded as a theory, is now a theory criticized and refuted; what stands firm is not its truth as theory, but the fact that it has actually been reached, the fact that we have experienced it; and in criticizing and demolishing it as a theory we are confirming and explaining it as an experience.

22. This, then, is the general nature of philosophical inference. The critical view of it was so far right, that it consists always and essentially in refutation; whatever positive doctrine has been propounded, the next step for philosophy is to demolish it, to destroy it as a theory, and leave it standing only as an experience. But this view only apprehends the negative side of the process; it misses the positive side, the necessity of explaining that experience by

reference to the new principles implied in the critical process itself.

The analytic view was so far right, that every movement of philosophical thought begins with a datum which is already knowledge, and goes on to explain what this knowledge means. It is only wrong because it forgets that, in explaining our knowledge, we come to know it in a different way; the datum does not remain a fixed point, it undergoes development in undergoing analysis, and therefore vanishes in its original form, to reappear in a new.

It is right to describe philosophical thought as deductive, because at every phase in its development it is, ideally at least, a complete system based on principles and connected throughout its texture by strict logical bonds; but this system is more than a deductive system, because the principles are open to criticism and must be defended by their success in explaining our experience.

For this reason, because philosophy is always an attempt to discern the principles which run through experience and make it a rational whole, it is right to call it inductive; but it differs from an inductive science because the experience on which its theories are based is itself an experience of rational living, theorizing, philosophizing. Consequently, because the data from which it begins and which it has to explain are homogeneous with its conclusions, the theories by which it seeks to explain them, the activity of philosophizing is a datum to philosophy, and among its tasks is the task of accounting for itself; and this, which is true even at a quite low level of philosophical development, is more and more so as it becomes more and more philosophical; so that the maturity of a philosophy may be judged by the clearness with which it apprehends the principle laid down at the beginning of this essay, that the theory of philosophy is an essential part of philosophy.

IX
THE IDEA OF SYSTEM
§ 1

1. In the first chapter of this essay it was remarked that the most recent constructive movement in philosophical thought, there called the Kantian, drew to its close a hundred years ago; that a time followed when philosophical studies sank into comparative insignificance and neglect; and that they are now reviving, and have reached a condition of ferment which appears to hold out hopes of a new constructive movement. Construction implies system; and in philosophy, which has among its necessary tasks the task of understanding itself, a period of constructive effort must be a time when thought conceives itself as essentially systematic in form. If therefore we are to hope for a future period of constructive work in philosophy, we must decide what we mean in such a context by constructive; that is, we must form a clear idea of the nature of a philosophical system.

Before we can do this, we must overcome a certain prejudice, natural to a time of ferment and experiment, and still more so to a time of apathy and neglect, against the idea of system in itself. This prejudice has become almost an orthodoxy in the last hundred years, when the idea of philosophy as a system has been, more often than not, either derided as an outgrown superstition or, if accepted, accepted only with apologies and qualifications.

It is not a mere prejudice. It is based on reasons, and serious reasons; the chief of them appear to be these.

It is said that the idea of system is incompatible with the conception of thought as constantly advancing through new discoveries to new points of view. A system claims finality; but there is no finality in human knowledge, and the philosopher who builds a system is only trying, and always trying in vain, to close the doors of the future. A system claims completeness; but however it may have been in the past when the total accumulation of knowledge in man's possession was small, the vastness of the field which must be covered by any general view of modern knowledge makes it an enterprise far beyond the powers of a single man. A system claims objectivity; but in effect it is only a personal and private thing, the expression of its author's subjective point of view: there are as many philosophical systems as there are philosophers; whereas the march of science has shown that the only hope of permanence lies in the humbler project of adding here a little and there a little to a body of knowledge that transcends the purview of any single contributor to the whole. And lastly, a system claims unity; it claims that every problem is connected with every other, and it claims to solve every problem by applying to it certain uniform rules of method; so that every question philosophy can raise is fitted or rather forced into a single mould, and accommodated to the architecture of a single building; whereas philosophy has problems so diverse in kind that they can only be handled satisfactorily if each is handled on its merits, with a freedom and suppleness of method far greater than any idea of system will allow.

2. It would be easy to answer these objections by criticizing them as an unstable compound formed of two elements : a certain hostility towards philosophy as such, resulting in a demand that it should either cease to exist or, if it must continue, renounce its old methods and its old aims and conform in both these respects to the pattern of science ; and a right appreciation of philosophy's true nature, and a demand that it should no longer be content to ape other forms of thought, but begin at last to pursue its own proper aims by its own proper methods. It would be easy to show that, so far as they are based on the first motive, they can be answered on the principles already laid down in this essay ; and that, so far as they are based on the second, they express an objection not to philosophical systems as such but to non-philosophical systems usurping their function, and claiming their name.

But this method of answering them would hardly do them justice. They are varying expressions of a demand which any future philosophy must satisfy, and a conviction that this demand has not been altogether satisfied by any philosophy of the past. This demand and this conviction could be expressed in a logical and coherent way only by some one already possessed of a logical and coherent philosophy ; but the objections I have outlined are felt by persons who would frankly disclaim any such possession; they are indeed a way of explaining why those who feel them neither have nor hope to have a philosophical system of their own. Such a criticism as I have outlined, therefore, would be a mere exhibition of pedantry: it would mean treating them as if they were the outcome of a systematic philosophy, which they do not profess to be, and at the same time failing to criticize or even to understand their spirit. In what follows, therefore, I shall endeavour to treat them as expressions of a point of view with which any future constructive philosophy that is more than an academic game must come to terms.

3. The first objection is that a system claims finality, and that this claim must always be false, since human knowledge is always growing and changing. Taken literally, this is an objection not to the idea of a philosophical system but to the idea of any system whatever, for example, a systematic presentation of mathematics or medicine; for in all fields of study there is always hope of new advance, and in none can a system, whenever it is formed, be final. In spite of this, scientists and historians and other students try to present their knowledge from time to time in a systematic form; and their systems, though bound to be superseded, serve a necessary purpose, not closing the doors of the future but rather opening them; for in order to advance in knowledge we must first know where we stand, and no student can take stock of his position without attempting to state it systematically.

But the objection does tell with special force against the idea of a philosophical system. In other fields of thought it is plausible, I do not ask how far it is ever really true, to describe our knowledge as an aggregate of separable items: an inventory, to which additions can be made without altering what was there before. Even when the addition is logically derived from what was there before, its deduction is an irreversible process which does not recoil upon its starting-point. In these fields, therefore, it is plausible to suggest that when we take stock of our knowledge we are reviewing assets that are permanent; whereas in philosophy, because every new discovery reacts upon what we knew before, the whole body of knowledge must be remade from the foundations at every step in advance.

All this may be granted; but although it proves that a philosophical system is peculiarly difficult to construct, it does not prove that the attempt to construct it is mistaken. After all, philosophy is a form of human thought, subject to change, liable to error, capable of progress. The philosopher therefore, like every student, must sum up his progress from time to time, and express his conclusions in a systematic form, if progress is to continue. Owing to certain peculiarities of philosophy, this demands more patience and a more critical outlook than the corresponding audit of history or science; but it cannot on that account be omitted. Nor does it in philosophy more than elsewhere imply a claim to finality. That must be recognized by all philosophies of the future. Not that it has been altogether overlooked by philosophies of the past; one of the greatest system-builders at the close of one of his systematic treatises wrote the words *bis hieher ist das Bewusstseyn gekommen*; and on this note—the past has been liquidated, we are now ready for the future—every system, philosophical or other, must end.

4. The second criticism was that to-day no single thinker can survey the entire field of knowledge so as to achieve that completeness of view which the construction of a philosophical system demands. That no one man can adequately survey the entire field of modern knowledge may be granted; but it does not follow that no one man can adequately survey the field of modern philosophy. The business of philosophy is not to be an encyclopaedia of human knowledge, but to deal with its own special problems in its own special way; and since philosophy less than any other branch of knowledge presents the appearance of an accumulation of facts, there is less reason in philosophy than anywhere else to think that the passage of time makes the subject unwieldy by sheer growth in bulk.

Yet even so, the objector may insist, the construction of a strictly philosophical system, with all the demands it makes upon its author both within and without the sphere of strictly philosophical knowledge, is a task beyond the powers of any one man. But it is a task which no one man is or ever has been called upon to discharge. The great systems of the past have always been built up by incorporating material drawn from the work of others; thus, instead of conceiving the history of thought as a succession of personal systems, a Socratic philosophy, a Platonic philosophy, an Aristotelian philosophy and so on, it would be nearer the truth to think of a single Greek philosophy, the work of many minds, remodelling and in part reconstructing it as successive generations of builders reconstructed a medieval church.

If every system stands thus in organic relation to the past, it stands in organic relation to the present also. Every philosopher finds himself shepherded, as it were, into a particular line of study by the fact that others round him are doing work which requires this as its complement; there is in philosophy, as in every science, a tacit partition of the field of thought, and the work of each thinker is his contribution to a wider whole in which he feels himself a collaborator.

Since every philosophy is in part a borrowing from philosophies of the past and in part a collaboration with those of the present, there can be no such thing as a private, personal, self-contained system. If it has ever in the past been fancied that this could be so, and that is a question of history which need not here be raised, the vanity is one that must be renounced for the future.

5. The third objection was that whereas, by its very nature as thought, philosophy claims objective validity, this is a claim which in its form as a system it can never make good. A philosophical system is regarded as essentially subjective, a personal and private thing, an expression of the way in which

its author looks at the world. Science, it is said, is impersonal and objective, so that its results are valid for all rational beings and for all time; a philosophical system is so bound up with subjective elements that none holds good beyond the limits of the mind that created it; and this defect, it is thought, can only be overcome by abandoning the idea of a systematic or comprehensive philosophy, and applying to philosophy the method of piecemeal study and accumulation of detailed results which has proved fruitful in the case of the sciences.

The idea of a personal and private system, I need not repeat, is one which I have no wish to defend. But this objection, in effect, drives home a supposed implication of what I have already said. 'Admit that each philosopher merely contributes his quota to the general advancement of philosophical thought,' it argues, 'and you give up the idea of system altogether. You cannot have it both ways; a system is one thing, a contribution towards a system is another; if each individual philosopher's task is to provide the latter, no philosopher is concerned to provide the former.'

But is not this the fallacy of false disjunction? The individual philosopher is certainly making his personal contribution to the advancement of thought, and that is all he can ever hope to do. But the thought to which he is contributing is philosophical thought; and this includes as an integral part of itself the theory of itself; hence every philosopher, in making this contribution, must think of himself as making it; that is, he must have his theory of his own contribution's place in the whole to which he is contributing. Hence, in making this personal contribution, he must reconsider the general question what philosophy is.

This, accordingly, is not a contradiction but a complement of what was said in answer to the second objection. It follows from the peculiar nature of philosophy that each philosopher, if he genuinely does make his own contribution to knowledge, cannot be merely adding another item to an inventory; he must be shaping afresh in his own mind the idea of philosophy as a whole. And conversely, it is only by attempting this task, formidable as it is, that he can make any contribution, however modest, to the general advancement of philosophy; for until he has confronted this problem the work which he is doing, whatever else it may be, is not genuinely philosophical work, since it lacks one of the distinctive marks of philosophical thinking.

6. The fourth objection was that the ideal of philosophy as a system does violence to the diversity of philosophical problems by forcing them into a single mould and constantly asserting connexions between them, when in point of fact they are better dealt with as independent problems, each to be considered on its merits and solved by methods appropriate to itself. The objector feels, rather than conceives, philosophy as the constant endeavour to solve problems that spring up spontaneously at this or that point all over the field of its subject-matter; each

problem presents new features both in content and in form, and requires a fresh eye and a flexible mind for its adequate solution; and all alike are sure to be falsely stated and falsely solved if approached from the starting-point of a ready-made formula.

A reader of this essay does not need to be told that rigid and ready-made formulae are fatal to sound philosophical method; if he accepts the general point of view developed in the preceding chapters, he will welcome this new objector as an ally. But he may be a dangerous one. If he only means that a philosopher must aim systematically and methodically at avoiding rigid formulae and at revising his principles in the light of his conclusions, well and good; but if he fails to see that a methodical avoidance of rigidity is itself a system of method, and thinks that there is no difference between systematic thought and thought in bondage to ready-made formulae, he is an anarchist of the mind, whose work can only lay waste the ground that thought has cultivated, and whose principles must not be allowed to pass unchallenged.

§ 2

7. I have met each of these four objections by conceding in principle the point for which the objector seemed anxious to contend; and the question next arises: after making all these concessions, what remains of the idea of system? Is not the anarchist right in thinking that philosophy can never hope to be in any intelligible sense of the word systematic, but must content itself with isolated discussions on

isolated points, each following a method improvised to fit the peculiarities of the subject-matter?

It will perhaps be best to answer this question in two stages: first by asking whether the proposal to abandon the idea of system in philosophy is a reasonable one, or whether it is not at bottom a self-contradiction, as if a man should say 'my method is to have no method; my one rule in thinking is to have no rules'; and then to ask whether the characteristics which have been admitted to belong to philosophical thought, so far from being inconsistent with the idea of system, may not be logical consequences of that idea when it is modified, according to the principles adopted elsewhere in this essay, to suit the special case of philosophy.

First, then, I think it can be shown that in some form or other the idea of system is inevitable in philosophy, and that no attempt to deny it can succeed unless it is pushed to the point of denying that the word philosophy has any meaning whatever.

Let us suppose that a philosopher, keenly alive to the differences between one problem and another, eager not to falsify any by assimilating it to one of another kind, and determined to treat each on its merits, lays down for himself the rule that every problem must be handled as if it had been the first and only problem that philosophical thought had ever encountered.

Now let him raise the question: what exactly, in rejecting the idea of system, am I rejecting? For example, am I denying that these various inquiries, sharing as they do the epithet philosophical, share some common nature whose name that epithet is? If to this question he replies that there is no such common nature, *cadit quaestio*; the word philosophy is a word without a meaning. But if there is a common nature, wherein does it consist?

It might consist in their form, as examples of the same general type of thinking, or in their content, as concerned with subject-matters of the same general kind. Suppose he places the community of nature in their form, that is already to abandon his position; for it implies that philosophical thought has its own ways of proceeding, so that the isolation of each problem from the rest in point of method disappears.

But the community of nature cannot be confined to form. In content or subject-matter, these various inquiries have this at least in common, that they are all concerned with philosophical topics. Thus the various subject-matters as well as the various methods, however widely they differ, must all alike be instances of philosophical subject-matter as well as philosophical method: they must in fact have that kind of relation to each other which connects instances of the same concept.

This concept is the concept of philosophy, in its formal aspect as the concept of philosophical thinking, and its material aspect as the concept of philosophical subjects or topics of thought. And this concept will, of course, be not only general but generic: it will divide into species and those into sub-species, thus forming a system of specifications into which it must be possible somewhere to fit any piece of philosophical thinking and any philosophical topic.

8. It should be possible to say more concerning the nature of this system. The concept of philosophy is itself a philosophical concept, and therefore its specific classes will overlap. It will be impossible to divide up the field of philosophical topics into mutually exclusive departments; ethical questions will show logical as well as ethical aspects, and vice versa; and the various philosophical sciences, instead of treating each a separate subject-matter of its own, should be regarded rather as treating each a distinct aspect of one and the same subject-matter. Spinoza, grappling with this problem, spoke of a single substance having two attributes, extension and thought, so related as to be not separable component parts of its essence, a false view into which it is easy to slip by speaking of aspects, but two languages, as it were, in each of which the whole nature of that substance is expressed. Two philosophical sciences dealing with extension and thought respectively would be concerned therefore, on Spinoza's view, not with two separate groups of topics, but with topics somehow at bottom the same.

It is very difficult to see how this sameness and this difference should be conceived; but clearly there are two ways in which it should not be conceived: there are not completely different groups of ethical, logical, &c., topics all having one identical philosophical form; nor is there one identical subject-matter in which all the differences between the different philosophical sciences are sunk into nothingness. The former misconception would divide the substance of philosophy, the latter would confound its distinctions.

9. Light can perhaps be thrown on these difficulties by advancing from the conception of overlapping classes to that of a scale of forms. If the concept of philosophy is a philosophical concept, different groups of philosophical topics will not only overlap, they will be philosophical in different ways and also to varying degrees; and the methods appropriate to them will correspondingly conform in different ways and in varying degrees to the general idea of philosophical method. The various parts which together make up the body of a philosophy will thus form a scale in whose ascent the subject-matter becomes progressively philosophical in the sense of coming more and more to be the kind of subject-matter of which philosophy is in search, and the method becomes progressively philosophical in the sense that it comes to exhibit more and more adequately the proper nature of philosophical thought.

From this point of view the conception of different philosophical sciences as treating distinct aspects of the same subject-matter, or expressing distinct attributes of one substance, will be modified by conceiving them as terms in a scale, each penetrating more deeply than the last into the essence of its subject-matter and expressing the nature of the one substance more adequately. Philosophy as a whole, in its form as a system, now appears as a scale of philosophies, each differing from the rest not only in kind, as dealing with a certain specific form of the one universal philosophical subject-matter by means of an appropriate and therefore specifically distinct method, but also in degree, as more or less adequately embodying the ideal of genuinely philosophical method applied to genuinely philosophical subject-matter.

Each form in such a scale sums up the whole scale to that point; that is to say, each form is itself a system in which the topics and methods of the subordinate forms find a subordinate place. From the point of view of a philosopher whose thought has reached a given form, each subordinate form, considered as a self-contained and distinct philosophy, presents two aspects. As a philosophy distinct from his own, it is a discussion by a method which he does not use of a problem with which he is not concerned; as a philosophy opposed to his own, it is a concrete example of how philosophizing should not be done. But this same form, when considered as subordinate to his own, appears as an error whose refutation he has already achieved; and, as something reabsorbed into his own, it constitutes an element within his own system; and thus one side of the task of all systematic philosophizing is to show the truth of theories which, considered as self-contained and distinct philosophies, would have to be condemned as errors.

10. The conception of systematic philosophy as a whole whose parts are related as terms in a scale of

forms, makes it possible to regard the four objections stated at the beginning of this chapter as together forming a rough and imperfect, but by no means inept, summary of the leading characteristics which a philosophical system should present.

'A philosophical system', it was said, 'claims finality, but the claim must always be false because the doors of the future are always open.' The contradiction vanishes when it is realized that the philosopher, in constructing a system, has his place in a scale whose structure is such that every term in it sums up the whole scale to that point; however far up the scale he goes, he never comes to an absolute end of the series, because by reaching this point he already comes in sight of new problems; but he is always at a relative end, in the sense that, wherever he stands, he must know where he stands and sum up his progress hitherto, on pain of making no progress henceforth. And every such summary can only be done once, and is therefore final: the problem which it must solve is finally solved.

'A philosophical system claims completeness; but in fact it can never be more than a contribution made by its author towards a wider synthesis.' Here again the notion of a scale of forms dispels the contradiction. As one form in a scale, an individual philosophy is one among many, a single moment in the history of thought, which future philosophers will have to treat as such; but as reinterpreting previous philosophies and reaffirming them as elements within itself it summarizes the whole previous course of that history, and is thus universal as well as individual.

'A philosophical system claims objectivity, but in fact it can only express its author's private and personal views.' Here again there is no contradiction, if the historical development of philosophy is regarded as the deployment of a scale of forms. So far as any man is a competent philosopher, his philosophy arises by objective necessity out of his situation in the history of thought and the problem with which he is confronted; but situation and problem are unique, and hence no one philosopher's system can be acceptable to another without some modification. That each must reject the thoughts of others, regarded as self-contained philosophies, and at the same time reaffirm them as elements in his own philosophy, is due not to causes in taste and temperament but to the logical structure of philosophical thought.

Lastly, 'a philosophical system claims uniformity of method, but a truly philosophical spirit will rather aim at flexibility.' But the flexibility that philosophy demands is not a random flexibility, a mere looseness in the application of a method nowhere quite appropriate; it is a uniform or methodical flexibility, in which the method changes from one topic to another because form and content are changing *pari passu* as thought, traversing its scale of forms, gradually approximates to the ideal of a perfectly philosophical subject-matter treated by a perfectly philosophical method.

Accordingly, these four contentions, instead of expressing the impossibility of any philosophical system, express the characteristics which any system must present if it is organized according to principles derived from the peculiar structure of the philosophical concept.

§ 3

11. Hitherto the idea of a philosophical system has been sketched, in the barest outline, merely as an idea, irrespectively of any realization of that idea in actual fact. Its characteristics have been merely deduced from the notion of a scale of forms. It remains to ask whether this ideal is anywhere and in any way realized.

That it is altogether unrealized we shall hardly expect, having already seen that an unrealized idea is a thing foreign to the essence of philosophical thought; the judgement that philosophy is essentially systematic is a categorical judgement, and means that whoever tries to think philosophically, and to some extent succeeds, must find and does find, when he reflects upon it, that his thought takes shape as a system. The idea of system is nowhere finally and completely realized; but it is always tending to realize itself wherever any diversity is recognized in the subject-matter and methods of thought. This constant tendency towards systematic shape finds expression in ways infinitely various: a new way, wherever philosophy finds a new kind of diversity to organize into a whole. Four examples will suffice.

12. First, the division of philosophy into the so-called philosophical sciences, metaphysics, logic, ethics, and so forth, is to some extent a realization of this idea; for to some extent these differ both in kind, as various ways of dealing with various kinds of problem, and in degree, as more and less philosophical treatments of topics more and less proper to philosophy. Every philosopher realizes that the subjects treated in these sciences are in some sense aspects of one and the same subject, and that both in subject and in method they form, however roughly, a scale, in which at one end there are subjects and methods hardly to be distinguished from those of empirical science—is psychology, for example, an empirical science or a philosophical?—and, at the other, perhaps in metaphysics, subjects in the strictest sense philosophical, treated by methods that in the highest degree exhibit the nature of philosophical thought. It is only in a rough and approximative way that the conventional canon of philosophical sciences corresponds to the idea of a system; but it is only in so far as it does correspond that it can claim philosophical importance; otherwise it represents a merely empirical grouping of philosophical topics.

13. Secondly, the history of philosophical thought, so far as it is a genuine history and not a merely temporal sequence of disconnected events, exhibits the same kind of approximation. It is a genuine history in so far as the events contained in it lead each to the next: so far, that is, as each philosopher has

learnt his philosophy through studying the work of his predecessors. For in that case each is trying to do what his predecessor did—to philosophize; but to do it better by doing it differently; assimilating whatever seems true, rejecting whatever seems false, and thus producing a new philosophy which is at the same time an improved version of the old. His successor in turn stands in this same relation to himself, and thus the entire history of thought is the history of a single sustained attempt to solve a single permanent problem, each phase advancing the problem by the extent of all the work done on it in the interval, and summing up the fruits of this work in the shape of a unique presentation of the problem. In a history of this kind all the philosophies of the past are telescoped into the present, and constitute a scale of forms, never beginning and never ending, which are different both in degree and in kind, distinct from each other and opposed to each other.

14. Thirdly, a philosopher might be asked to give some account of the state of philosophy in his own time; and it would be highly unphilosophical in him to reply that in his time there was no such thing as a state of philosophy, but only a chaos or babel of different philosophies; for this would show that he was either unwilling or unable to sort these philosophies into their kinds, to analyse their affinities, and to assess their merits. To a philosophical eye these various relations are not given to their terms from without, by the arbitrary act of a systematizing intellect; they really subsist in and between the

terms, and to apprehend the terms without apprehending these relations is to misapprehend them. But if these relations are grasped, I do not say completely, for completion is here as in all philosophical enterprises unattainable, but to any considerable degree, the philosophical views between which they subsist will reveal themselves as nodal points in a system of thought which, as a whole, may be called the philosophy of the present day.

This system cannot be conceived except as a scale of forms; for the various philosophies which go to compose it vary in the degree to which they deserve the title philosophy of the present day; some are too unphilosophical to claim that title without qualification, some too antiquated, some too fragmentary, some too negative; each presents a double aspect, partly as an attempt, never quite successful, at a complete philosophy, partly as a contribution to something wider than itself; but ideally a place can be found even for the crudest and least philosophical of them in a scale which, travelling downward towards zero but never reaching it, is long enough to accommodate all those dim and fluctuating half-philosophical and quarter-philosophical opinions out of which, partly by consolidation and partly by criticism, there emerges the comparatively definite and organized group of theories collectively called the philosophy of to-day. With that emergence the second main phase of the scale is reached. The third is reached when these organized and ostensibly conflicting theories are shown to participate according to their degrees and kinds in a single common spirit which, not in a collective but in an eminent sense, is the philosophy of the present.

Such a system is only an ideal, in the sense that it regulates the procedure of a philosopher trying to answer the question at issue, and cannot be expected to present itself fully formed in his answer; but it is not an ideal imposed on his subject-matter by his thought; it is the way in which he must apprehend his subject-matter if he is to apprehend it correctly.

15. Lastly, he undertakes a task not very different from this when he tries to think out his own philosophy. He begins by finding in himself a welter of half-philosophical and quarter-philosophical opinions not at bottom, if he will consider them candidly, more harmonious with each other than those of different contemporary persons; out of these, which already vary in his estimate of their importance and profundity, there emerge once more by consolidation and criticism certain more or less definitely philosophical positions; these again vary in the conviction with which they are held, some merely played with, some maintained with diffidence, some judged fundamental, but each liable on examination to prove contradictory with some of the rest. The process now begins again at a higher level, and he tries to see these various positions as parts of a connected whole, or, failing that, to correct the recalcitrant elements until they fall into place; this implies not only adjusting the parts to the idea of the whole but adjusting the idea of the whole to meet the demands

of the parts, so that the idea of the whole is itself undergoing transformation as the scale is traversed upwards.

These are only examples of innumerable ways in which philosophical thought tends to organize itself into a system having the general character of a scale of forms. What is permanent and essential is not this or that system, for every particular system is nothing but an interim report on the progress of thought down to the time of making it, but the necessity of thinking systematically; and although this necessity may be overlooked or denied with no great harm done so long as philosophy aims only at being negative or critical, or attempts no more than desultory and short-winded constructive flights, in order to do its proper work properly it must understand what that work is: in other words, philosophy must think of itself as systematic.

X
PHILOSOPHY AS A BRANCH OF LITERATURE

§ 1

1. PHILOSOPHY is a name that belongs not only to a certain realm of thought, but also to the literature in which that thought finds or seeks expression. It belongs to the subject of this essay, therefore, if only by way of appendix, to ask whether philosophical literature has any peculiarities corresponding to those of the thought which it tries to express.

Literature as a genus is divided into the species poetry and prose. Prose is marked by a distinction between matter and form: what we say and how we say it. The formal elements are those which we call literary quality, style, writing, and so forth; the material elements are what we generally call the 'contents' of the work. Each part has its own scale of values. On its formal side, prose should be clear, expressive, and in the most general sense of that word beautiful; on its material side, it should be well thought out, intelligent, and in a general sense true. To satisfy the first claim the prose writer must be an artist; to satisfy the second, he must be a thinker.

2. These parts are distinct, but they cannot be separated. As elements in prose, neither can exist without the other. If it were possible for a book to be well thought out but ill written, it would not be

literature at all; if it could be well written but ill thought out, it would at any rate not be prose. But the two do not exist in equilibrium. The formal part is the servant of the material. We speak well, in prose, only in order to say what we mean: the matter is prior to the form. This priority, no doubt, is rather logical than temporal. The matter does not exist as a naked but fully formed thought in our minds before we fit it with a garment of words. It is only in some dark and half-conscious way that we know our thoughts before we come to express them. Yet in that obscure fashion they are already within us; and, rising into full consciousness as we find the words to utter them, it is they that determine the words, not vice versa.

3. In poetry, this distinction between matter and form does not exist. Instead of two linked problems, finding out what he wants to say and finding out how to say it, the poet has only one problem. Instead of having to satisfy two standards of value, beauty and truth, the poet recognizes only one. The sole business of a poem is to be beautiful; its sole merits are formal or literary merits. In the sense in which the prose writer is trying to say something, there is nothing that the poet is trying to say; he is trying simply to speak.

4. Prose and poetry are philosophically distinct species of a genus; consequently they overlap. Literary excellence, which is the means to an end in prose and the sole end or essence of poetry, is the same thing in both cases. Judged by a purely literary or

artistic standard, the merits of even the best prose are inferior to those of even commonplace poetry; for these qualities are of necessity degraded in becoming means instead of ends; yet the prose writer does inhabit the mountain of poetry, though he lives only on its lower slopes, and drinks of its waters not fresh from their spring but muddy with the silt of their stream-beds.

5. This distinction must not be confused with the distinction between prose and verse, which is an empirical division between two ways of writing, either of which may be poetical or prosaic in character. There is no doubt a tendency for poetry to take the outward shape of verse; that is because verse, in its patterns of rhythm and rhyme, expresses a native tendency on the part of language to organize itself according to intrinsic formal characters whenever it is liberated from the task of expressing thought. Similar formal patterns are always emerging in the structure of prose, only to be lost again; they emerge because without them language would be wholly non-poetical and would therefore cease to be language; they are lost again because form is here subordinate to matter, and the poetry inherent in language is therefore shattered into an infinity of inchoate poems.

§ 2

6. Philosophy as a kind of literature belongs to the realm of prose. But within that realm it has certain characteristics of its own, which can best be

seen by comparing it with the literatures of science and of history.

Scientific literature contains, as a noteworthy element in its vocabulary, a number of technical terms. If the scientist were refused permission to use these terms, he could not express his strictly scientific thoughts at all; by using them more and more freely, he comes to express himself with greater and greater ease and sureness. In philosophical literature, technical terms are regarded with some suspicion. They are slightingly described as jargon, and philosophers who use them much are derided as pedants or criticized for evading the duty of explaining themselves and the even more urgent duty of understanding themselves.

This impression of a difference between the ideals of a scientific vocabulary and a philosophical is only deepened by observing that many of the greatest philosophers, especially those who by common consent have written well in addition to thinking well, have used nothing that can be called a technical vocabulary. Berkeley has none; Plato none, if consistency of usage is a test; Descartes none, except when he uses a technical term to point a reference to the thoughts of others; and where a great philosopher like Kant seems to revel in them, it is by no means agreed that his thought gains proportionately in precision and intelligibility, or that the stylist in him is equal to the philosopher.

A general review of the history of philosophy compared with the equally long history of mathe matics, would show that whereas exact science has from the first been at pains to build up a technical vocabulary in which every term should have a rigid and constant meaning, philosophy has always taken a different road: its terms have shifted their meaning from one writer to another, and in successive phases of the same writer's work, in a way which is the exact opposite of what we find in science, and would justify the assertion that, in the strict sense of the word technical, philosophy has never had anything that deserved the name of a technical vocabulary.

Before concluding that this is a state of things calling for amendment, it may be well to ask what technical terms are, and why they are needed in the expression of scientific thought.

7. Technical terms are terms not used in ordinary speech, but invented *ad hoc* for a special purpose, or else they are borrowed from ordinary speech but used *ad hoc* in a special sense. They are needed because it is desired to express a thought for whose expression ordinary speech does not provide. Hence, because they are essentially innovations in vocabulary, and artificial or arbitrary innovations, they cannot be understood and therefore must not be used unless they are defined: and definition, here, means 'verbal' as distinct from 'real' definition.

It has sometimes been maintained that all language consists of sounds taken at pleasure to serve as marks for certain thoughts or things: which would amount to saying that it consists of technical terms. But since a technical term implies a definition, it is impossible that all words should be technical terms, for if they were we could never understand their definitions. The business of language is to express or explain; if language cannot explain itself, nothing else can explain it; and a technical term, in so far as it calls for explanation, is to that extent not language but something else which resembles language in being significant, but differs from it in not being expressive or self-explanatory. Perhaps I may point the distinction by saying that it is properly not a word but a symbol, using this term as when we speak of mathematical symbols. The technical vocabulary of science is thus neither a language nor a special part of language, but a symbolism like that of mathematics. It presupposes language, for the terms of which it consists are intelligible only when defined, and they must be defined in ordinary or non-technical language, that is, in language proper. But language proper does not presuppose technical terms, for in poetry, where language is most perfectly and purely itself, no technical terms are either used or presupposed, any more than in the primitive speech of childhood or the ordinary speech of conversation.

Thus the technical element in scientific language is an element foreign to the essence of language as such. So far as scientific literature allows itself to be guided by its natural tendency to rely on technical terms, scientific prose falls apart into two things: expressions, as a mathematician speaks of expressions, made up of technical terms, which signify scientific thought but are not language, and the verbal definitions of these terms, which are language but do not signify scientific thought.

8. Philosophical literature shows no such tendency. Even when, owing to the mistaken idea that whatever is good in science will prove good in philosophy, it has tried to imitate science in this respect, the imitation has been slight and superficial, and the further it has gone the less good it has done. This is because the peculiar necessity for a technical vocabulary in science has no counterpart in philosophy.

Technical terms are needed in science because in the course of scientific thought we encounter concepts which are wholly new to us, and for which therefore we must have wholly new names. Such words as chiliagon and pterodactyl are additions to our vocabulary because the things for which they stand are additions to our experience. This is possible because the concepts of science are divided into mutually exclusive species, and consequently there can be specifications of a familiar genus which are altogether new to us.

In philosophy, where the species of a genus are not mutually exclusive, no concept can ever come to us as an absolute novelty; we can only come to know better what to some extent we knew already. We therefore never need an absolutely new word for an absolutely new thing. But we do constantly need relatively new words for relatively new things: words with which to indicate the new aspects, new distinctions, new connexions which thought brings to light in a familiar subject-matter; and even these are not so much new to us as hitherto imperfectly apprehended.

This demand cannot be satisfied by technical terms. On the contrary, technical terms, owing to their rigidity and artificiality, are a positive impediment to its satisfaction. In order to satisfy it, a vocabulary needs two things: groups of words nearly but not quite synonymous, differentiated by shades of meaning which for some purposes can be ignored and for others become important; and single words which, without being definitely equivocal, have various senses distinguished according to the ways in which they are used.

9. These two characteristics are precisely those which ordinary language, as distinct from a technical vocabulary, possesses. It is easy to verify this statement by comparing the scientific definition of such a word as circle with the account given for example in the *Oxford English Dictionary* of what the same word means or may mean in ordinary usage. If it is argued, according to the method followed elsewhere in this essay, that since technical terms are used in science something corresponding to them, *mutatis mutandis*, will be found in philosophy, the modifications necessary to change the concept of a technical term from the shape appropriate to science into the shape appropriate to philosophy will deprive it exactly of what makes it a technical term and convert it into ordinary speech.

The language of philosophy is therefore, as every careful reader of the great philosophers already knows, a literary language and not a technical. Wherever a philosopher uses a term requiring formal definition, as distinct from the kind of exposition described in the fourth chapter, the intrusion of a non-literary element into his language corresponds with the intrusion of a non-philosophical element into his thought: a fragment of science, a piece of inchoate philosophizing, or a philosophical error; three things not, in such a case, easily to be distinguished.

The duty of the philosopher as a writer is therefore to avoid the technical vocabulary proper to science, and to choose his words according to the rules of literature. His terminology must have that expressiveness, that flexibility, that dependence upon context, which are the hall-marks of a literary use of words as opposed to a technical use of symbols.

A corresponding duty rests with the reader of philosophical literature, who must remember that he is reading a language and not a symbolism. He must neither think that his author is offering a verbal definition when he is making some statement about the essence of a concept—a fertile source of sophistical criticisms—nor complain when nothing resembling such a definition is given; he must expect philosophical terms to express their own meaning by the way in which they are used, like the words of ordinary speech. He must not expect one word always to mean one thing in the sense that its meaning undergoes no kind of change; he must expect philosophical terminology, like all language, to be always in process of development, and he must recollect that this, so far from making it harder to understand, is what makes it able to express its own meaning instead of being incomprehensible apart from definitions, like a collection of rigid and therefore artificial technical terms.

§ 3

10. In using words as words, that is, in writing literary or artistic prose, the philosopher resembles the historian. But here again there are differences. Expounding a concept and narrating a sequence of events both demand artistic writing; but the difference in subject-matter entails a corresponding difference in style.

Historical writing is an attempt to communicate to the reader something which the writer selects for communication out of his store of knowledge. He never tries to write down all he knows about his subject, but only a part of it. Indeed, this is all he can do. Events in time fall outside one another; but they are connected by chains of consequence; and therefore, since those we know are linked in this way with others which we do not know, there is always a certain element of incomprehensibility even in those we know best. Therefore our knowledge of any given fact is incomplete; because it is incomplete, we cannot say how incomplete it is; and all we can be sure of is some central nucleus of knowledge, beyond which there extends in every direction a penumbra of uncertainty. In historical writing, what we aim at doing is to express this nucleus of knowledge, ignoring the uncertainties that lie outside it. We try to steer clear of doubts and problems, and stick to what is certain. This division of what we know into what we know for certain and what we know in a doubtful or problematic way, the first being narrated and the second suppressed, gives every historical writer an air of knowing more than he says, and addressing himself to a reader who knows less than he. All historical writing is thus primarily addressed to a reader, and a relatively uninformed reader; it is therefore instructive or didactic in style. The reader is kept at arm's length, and is never admitted into the intimacy of the writer's mind; the writer, however conscientiously he cites authorities, never lays bare the processes of thought which have led him to his conclusions, because that would defer the completion of his narrative to the Greek calends, while he discussed his own states of consciousness, in which the reader is not interested.

11. Philosophy is in this respect the opposite of history. Every piece of philosophical writing is primarily addressed by the author to himself. Its purpose is not to select from among his thoughts those of which he is certain and to express those, but the very opposite: to fasten upon the difficulties and obscurities in which he finds himself involved, and try, if not to solve or remove them, at least to understand them better. The philosopher is forced to work in this way by the inextricable unity of the

object which he studies; it is not dispersed over space, as in physics, or over time, as in history; it is not a genus cut up into mutually exclusive species, or a whole whose parts can be understood separately; in thinking of it, therefore, he must always be probing into the darkest parts, as a guide trying to keep his party together must always be hastening the hindmost. The philosopher therefore, in the course of his business, must always be confessing his difficulties, whereas the historian is always to some extent concealing them. Consequently the difference between the writer's position and the reader's, which is so clear in historical literature, and is the cause of its didactic manner, does not exist in the literature of philosophy. The philosophers who have had the deepest instinct for style have repeatedly shrunk from adopting the form of a lecture or instructive address, and chosen instead that of a dialogue in which the work of self-criticism is parcelled out among the dramatis personae, or a meditation in which the mind communes with itself, or a dialectical process where the initial position is modified again and again as difficulties in it come to light.

Common to all these literary forms is the notion of philosophical writing as essentially a confession, a search by the mind for its own failings and an attempt to remedy them by recognizing them. Historians may be pardoned, even praised, for a slightly dogmatic and hectoring tone, a style calculated to deepen the sense of division between themselves and their readers, an attempt to impress and convince. Philosophers are debarred from these methods. Their only excuse for writing is that they mean to make a clean breast, first to themselves, and then to their readers, if they have any. Their style must be the plain and modest style proper to confession, a style not devoid of feeling, yet devoid of the element of bombast which sits not ungracefully upon the historian. They must sedulously avoid the temptation to impress their readers with a sense of inferiority in learning or ingenuity to their authors. They must never instruct or admonish; or at least, they must never instruct or admonish their readers, but only themselves.

12. There is accordingly a difference in attitude towards what he reads between the reader of historical literature and the reader of philosophical. In reading the historians, we 'consult' them. We apply to the store of learning in their minds for a grant of knowledge to make good the lack in our own. We do not seek to follow the processes of thought by which they came to know these things; we can only do that by becoming equally accomplished historians ourselves, and this we cannot do by reading their books, but only by working as they have worked at the original sources. In reading the philosophers, we 'follow' them: that is, we understand what they think, and reconstruct in ourselves, so far as we can, the processes by which they have come to think it. There is an intimacy in the latter relation which can never exist in the former. What we demand of the historian is a product of his thought; what we demand of the philosopher is his thought itself. The reader of a

philosophical work is committing himself to the enterprise of living through the same experience that his author lived through; if for lack of sympathy, patience, or any other quality he cannot do this, his reading is worthless.

§ 4

13. In this respect philosophy resembles poetry; for in poetry also the writer confesses himself to the reader, and admits him to the extremest intimacy. Hence the two things are sometimes confused, especially by persons who look upon each with suspicion as an outrage on the privacy of the individual mind; and because the resemblance becomes increasingly evident as philosophy becomes increasingly philosophical, this hostility singles out the greatest philosophers for peculiar obloquy, and finds in their writing a mere expression of emotion, or poem.

Even granting the justice of that description, it is incomplete. A philosophical work, if it must be called a poem, is not a mere poem, but a poem of the intellect. What is expressed in it is not emotions, desires, feelings, as such, but those which a thinking mind experiences in its search for knowledge; and it expresses these only because the experience of them is an integral part of the search, and that search is thought itself. When this qualification is added, it becomes plain that philosophical literature is in fact prose; it is poetry only in the sense in which all prose is poetry—poetry modified by the presence of a content, something which the writer is trying to say.

14. What explains the confusion is that philosophy represents the point at which prose comes nearest to being poetry. Owing to the unique intimacy of the relation between the philosophical writer among prose writers and his reader, a relation which elsewhere exists only in fine art or in the wide sense of that word poetry, there is a constant tendency for philosophy as a literary *genre* to overlap with poetry along their common frontier. Many of the greatest philosophers, and notably those among them who have been the best writers and therefore ought to know in what style to write philosophy, have adopted an imaginative and somewhat poetic style which would have been perverse in science and ridiculous in history but in philosophy is often highly successful. The dialogue form of Plato, where philosophies come to life as dramatic characters, the classical elegance of Descartes, the lapidary phrases of Spinoza, the tortured metaphor-ridden periods of Hegel, are neither defects in philosophical expression nor signs of defects in philosophical thought; they are signal instances of a tendency that is universal in philosophical literature, and to which it yields in proportion as its thought is more profound and its expression more adequate.

15. This provides a clue to the main principle which must be followed in learning to write philosophy, as distinct from learning to think it. Quite

otherwise than the scientist, and far more than the historian, the philosopher must go to school with the poets in order to learn the use of language, and must use it in their way: as a means of exploring one's own mind, and bringing to light what is obscure and doubtful in it. This, as the poets know, implies skill in metaphor and simile, readiness to find new meanings in old words, ability in case of need to invent new words and phrases which shall be understood as soon as they are heard, and briefly a disposition to improvise and create, to treat language as something not fixed and rigid but infinitely flexible and full of life.

The principles on which the philosopher uses language are those of poetry; but what he writes is not poetry but prose. From the point of view of literary form, this means that whereas the poet yields himself to every suggestion that his language makes, and so produces word-patterns whose beauty is a sufficient reason for their existence, the philosopher's word-patterns are constructed only to reveal the thought which they express, and are valuable not in themselves but as means to that end. The prose-writer's art is an art that must conceal itself, and produce not a jewel that is looked at for its own beauty but a crystal in whose depths the thought can be seen without distortion or confusion; and the philosophical writer in especial follows the trade not of a jeweller but of a lens-grinder. He must never use metaphors or imagery in such a way that they attract to themselves the attention due to his thought;

if he does that he is writing not prose, but, whether well or ill, poetry; but he must avoid this not by rejecting all use of metaphors and imagery, but by using them, poetic things themselves, in the domestication of prose: using them just so far as to reveal thought, and no farther.

§ 5

16. The reader, on his side, must approach his philosophical author precisely as if he were a poet, in the sense that he must seek in his work the expression of an individual experience, something which the writer has actually lived through, and something which the reader must live through in his turn by entering into the writer's mind with his own. To this basic and ultimate task of following or understanding his author, coming to see what he means by sharing his experience, the task of criticizing his doctrine, or determining how far it is true and how far false, is altogether secondary. A good reader, like a good listener, must be quiet in order to be attentive; able to refrain from obtruding his own thoughts, the better to apprehend those of the writer; not passive, but using his activity to follow where he is led, not to find a path of his own. A writer who does not deserve this silent, uninterrupting attention does not deserve to be read at all.

17. In reading poetry this is all we have to do; but in reading philosophy there is something else. Since the philosopher's experience consisted in, or at least arose out of, the search for truth, we must

ourselves be engaged in that search if we are to share the experience; and therefore, although our attitude to philosophy and poetry, simply as expressions, is the same, our attitude towards them differs in that philosophy expresses thought, and in order to share that experience we must ourselves think.

It is not enough that we should in a general way be thoughtful or intelligent; not enough even that we should be interested and skilled in philosophy. We must be equipped, not for any and every philosophical enterprise, but for the one which we are undertaking. What we can get by reading any book is conditioned by what we bring to it; and in philosophy no one can get much good by reading the works of a writer whose problems have not already arisen spontaneously in the reader's mind. Admitted to the intimacy of such a man's thought, he cannot follow it in its movement, and soon loses sight of it altogether and may fall to condemning it as illogical or unintelligible, when the fault lies neither in the writer's thought nor in his expression, nor even in the reader's capacities, but only in the reader's preparation. If he lays down the book, and comes back to it ripened by several years of philosophical labour, he may find it both intelligible and convincing.

These are the two conditions on which alone a reader can follow or understand a philosophical writer: one relating to the reader's aesthetic or literary education or his fitness to read books in general, the other to his philosophical education as fitting him to read this particular book. But in addition to understanding his author, the reader must criticize him.

18. Comprehension and criticism, or understanding what the writer means and asking whether it is true, are distinct attitudes, but not separable. The attempt to comprehend without criticizing is in the last resort a refusal to share in one essential particular the experience of the writer; for he has written no single sentence, if he is worth reading, without asking himself 'is that true?', and this critical attitude to his own work is an essential element in the experience which we as his readers are trying to share. If we refuse to criticize, therefore, we are making it impossible for ourselves to comprehend. That conversely it is impossible to criticize without comprehending is a principle which needs no defence.

Though the two cannot be separated, however, one is prior to the other: the question whether a man's views are true or false does not arise until we have found out what they are. Hence the reader's thought must always move from comprehension to criticism: he must begin by postponing criticism, although he knows it will come, and devote himself entirely to the task of comprehending; just as the writer, however ready and able to criticize himself, must begin by framing to himself some statement of what he thinks, or he will have nothing on which to exercise his self-criticism.

There is accordingly no contradiction between saying that comprehension is inseparable from criticism, and saying that a good reader must keep quiet and refrain from obtruding his own thoughts when trying to understand his author. Comprehension is inseparable from criticism in the sense that the one necessarily leads to the other, and reaches its own completion only in that process; but in this development, as in all others, we must begin at the beginning; and the first phase of the process is a phase in which criticism is latent. In this phase the reader must refrain from obtruding his own thoughts, not because he ought to have none of his own, but because at this stage his author's are more important: criticism is not forbidden, it is only postponed.

19. Granted, then, that the preliminary question what the author means is answered, and the reader is qualified to begin criticizing, how should he proceed? Not by seeking for points of disagreement, however well founded. If criticism must go with comprehension, and if comprehension means sharing the author's experience, criticism cannot be content with mere disagreement; and in fact, whenever we find a critic systematically contradicting everything his author says, we are sure that he has failed to understand him. There are no doubt occasions on which a reader may say of a book, 'for my part, I do not propose to spend time on it; it seems to me a mere tissue of errors and confusions.' But this is not criticism. Criticism does not begin until the reader has overcome this attitude, and has submitted to the discipline of following the author's thought and reconstructing in himself the point of

view from which it proceeds. When this has been done, any rejection is of necessity qualified by certain concessions, a certain degree of sympathy and even of assent.

This implies that criticism has two sides, a positive and a negative, neither of which can be altogether absent if it is to be genuine or intelligent. The critic is a reader raising the question whether what he reads is true. In order to answer this question he must disentangle the true elements in the work he is criticizing from the false. If he thinks it contains no true elements, or that it contains no false, that is as much as to say he finds in it no work for a critic to do. The critic is a reader who agrees with his author's views up to a certain point, and on that limited agreement builds his case for refusing a completer agreement.

The critic must therefore work from within. His negative position is based on his positive: his primary work is to supplement his author's partial account of some matter by adding certain aspects which the author has overlooked; but, since the parts of a philosophical theory never stand to one another in a relation of mere juxtaposition, the omission of one part will upset the balance of the whole and distort the remaining parts; so his additions will entail some correction even of those elements which he accepts as substantially true.

20. Criticism, when these two aspects of it are considered together, may be regarded as a single operation: the bringing to completeness of a theory

which its author has left incomplete. So understood, the function of the critic is to develop and continue the thought of the writer criticized. Theoretically, the relation between the philosophy criticized and the philosophy that criticizes it is the relation between two adjacent terms in a scale of forms, the forms of a single philosophy in its historical development; and in practice, it is well known that a man's best critics are his pupils, and his best pupils the most critical.

XI
CONCLUSION

1. The reader who has had patience to follow me hither will now, at the close of my argument, remind me of the terms of our compact. In the second chapter I invited him to read on, if he was willing to accept for the sake of argument the hypothesis that traditional philosophy is right in regarding its concepts as specified, unlike those of exact and empirical science, into overlapping classes. If he has accepted that invitation, it was on the understanding that we should see where the hypothesis led us: whether to an account of philosophical method consistent with itself and with our experience of philosophical thinking, or to a tissue of cobwebs, a house of cards, a castle in the air, or whatever phrase best describes the outcome of perverse and misguided reasoning. The time has now come to make a reckoning; that is my side of the agreement.

Beginning with the question how, on the assumption that they are to overlap, the species of a philosophical genus can be related to each other and to the genus, I tried to show that the condition would be satisfied if every philosophical concept were articulated into a scale of forms where each term differed from the next in a peculiar way combining differences of degree and kind, distinction and opposition. If this is so, the problem of defining a concept is not how to find a single phrase determining its genus and differentia, but how to express its whole content, beginning at the bottom of its scale of forms, in a reasoned and orderly definition coextensive and identical with a complete exposition of that concept. It would also follow that a philosophical judgement must be an organic whole in which affirmation and negation, universality, particularity, and singularity are all present; and that it cannot be devoid of a categorical or existential element. With regard to inference, it would follow that in philosophy this could be neither strictly deductive nor strictly inductive, but must consist in a deepening and widening of our knowledge, transforming it into a higher term on the same scale of forms; and lastly, after showing in what sense philosophy on this assumption could and must be a systematic whole, I tried to argue that there are certain consequences for the writer and reader of philosophical literature.

That this is a complete account of philosophical method I do not for a moment profess; what I have written is an essay, not a treatise. But so far as it goes, I hope it is consistent with itself. Whether my hopes are justified is a question I must now leave with the reader. It must also be asked, whether it is consonant with experience.

2. At this point I must make a confession, though it betrays no secret that the reader has not long ago discovered. The question whether this general view of philosophical thought agrees with experience is a question which I have not postponed until now, as the original terms of the compact might seem to

suggest; I have been putting it piecemeal at every step in the argument, which has always moved forward in two parallel lines, asking on the one hand 'what follows from our premisses?' and on the other 'what do we find in actual experience?' This double procedure, whose reasons could not be set forth until the eighth chapter, is the only one that can be either adopted or defended by any philosopher who has realized the deadliness of Hume's attack on what Kant was to call the dialectic of pure reason. 'Though the chain of arguments which conduct to it were ever so logical, there must arise a strong suspicion, if not an absolute assurance, that it has carried us quite beyond the reach of our faculties, when it leads to conclusions so extraordinary, and so remote from common life and experience. We are got into fairy land long ere we have reached the last steps of our theory; and *there* we have no reason to trust our common methods of argument, or to think that our usual analogies or probabilities have any authority. Our line is too short to fathom such immense abysses.'

For myself, though I could never plead guilty to a charge of scepticism, I am too diffident of my own reasoning powers to believe that I can neglect Hume's warning; and I know of no way in which I can travel in the wilds of philosophical thought except by this double method: compass and dead-reckoning, and the finding of my daily position by the stars.

3. But whose is this experience, the reader will

ask, by reference to which the argument professes to be checked? I can only reply: it is the experience of those who have worked at philosophy; the experience of others, as recorded in their writings, and our own, as preserved in our memory. This experience, embodied in the history of European thought, extends over twenty-five centuries, including the pre-Socratics at one end and the reader and myself at the other. To a person who does not understand what philosophy is, or by what processes it moves, the history of those sixty generations appears as a chaos, the record of random movements hither and thither by wandering planets, which no theory of epicycles can reduce to reason. But this appearance of irrationality, I make bold to say, cannot survive the discovery that philosophical thought has a structure of its own, and the hypothesis that in its changes it is obeying the laws of that structure. Thus, from the point of view of a rational theory of philosophy, the past history of philosophical thought no longer appears as irrational; it is a body of experience to which we can appeal with confidence, because we understand the principles at work in it, and in the light of those principles find it intelligible.

4. Is this a circular argument? Am I first deriving from philosophical tradition a certain view concerning the nature of philosophical thought, and then finding confirmation of that view in the fact of its agreement with tradition? And is it not doubly circular, since apart from my assuming that view the witness whose word confirms it would be dumb?

For, except on the assumption I have put forward, tradition, instead of an audible voice, is only a chaos of discordant ravings.

This is one of the ultimate questions which in the opening chapter of the present essay I undertook to avoid. I shall therefore answer it only obliquely, since a direct answer is ἄλλης σκέψεως οἰκειότερον.[1]

5. Assumption for assumption, which are we to prefer? That in sixty generations of continuous thought philosophers have been exerting themselves wholly in vain, and have waited for the first word of good sense until we came on the scene? Or that this labour has been on the whole profitable, and its history the history of an effort neither contemptible nor unrewarded? There is no one who does not prefer the second; and those who seem to have abandoned it in favour of the first have done so not from conceit but from disappointment. They have tried to see the history of thought as a history of achievement and progress; they have failed; and they have deserted their original assumption for another which no one, unless smarting under that experience, could contemplate without ridicule and disgust.

Yet it is surely in such a crisis as this that we should be most careful in choosing our path. The natural scientist, beginning with the assumption that nature is rational, has not allowed himself to be turned from that assumption by any of the difficulties into which it has led him; and it is because he

[1] The reader who is curious concerning this direct answer will find it given by implication in ch. viii, § 5. 20–21.

has regarded that assumption as not only legitimate but obligatory that he has won the respect of the whole world. If the scientist is obliged to assume that nature is rational, and that any failure to make sense of it is a failure to understand it, the corresponding assumption is obligatory for the historian, and this not least when he is the historian of thought.

So far from apologizing, therefore, for assuming that there is such a thing as the tradition of philosophy, to be discovered by historical study, and that this tradition has been going on sound lines, to be appreciated by philosophical criticism, I would maintain that this is the only assumption which can be legitimately made. Let it, for the moment, be called a mere assumption; at least I think it may be claimed that on this assumption the history of philosophy, properly studied and analysed, confirms the hope which I expressed in the first chapter: that by reconsidering the problem of method and adopting some such principles as are outlined in this essay, philosophy may find an issue from its present state of perplexity, and set its feet once more on the path of progress.

INDEX